MINI CRISS CROSS PUZZLES

D0878236

FRANCIS HEANEY

PUZZLE
WRIGHT
PRESS

New York

PUZZLE
WRIGHT
PRESS
New York

An Imprint of Sterling Publishing Co., Inc.
1166 Avenue of the Americas
New York, NY 10036

Also published in 2019 as *Large Print Crisscross Puzzles*

ISBN 978-1-4549-3028-0

Distributed in Canada by Sterling Publishing Co., Inc.
C/o Canadian Manda Group, 664 Annette Street
Toronto, Ontario M6S 2C8, Canada
Distributed in the United Kingdom by GMC Distribution Services
Castle Place, 166 High Street, Lewes, East Sussex BN7 1XU, England
Distributed in Australia by NewSouth Books
University of New South Wales, Sydney, NSW 2052, Australia

For information about custom editions, special sales, and premium
and corporate purchases, please contact Sterling Special Sales
at 800-805-5489 or specialsales@sterlingpublishing.com.

Manufactured in Canada

2   4   6   8   10   9   7   5   3   1

sterlingpublishing.com
puzzlewright.com

Cover design by Igor Satanovsky
Cover background image by elic/Shutterstock.com

CONTENTS

INTRODUCTION

Crisscrosses are some of the first puzzles that I remember solving when I was a kid. Back then, I started out mostly liking word puzzles, but soon started to solve logic puzzles as well. It wasn't until much later that I realized something: Crisscrosses are actually logic puzzles disguised as word puzzles! The process of solving a crisscross is one of careful analysis. You compare your list of entries to the empty grid, look at which words have certain letters in specific positions, discard the ones that won't work, and continue until you find the unique arrangement of words that fit in the grid. Having an instinct for language certainly helps, but the process is as logical (and as natural) as solving a sudoku. Where the word puzzle aspect comes into play is in the puzzle themes. Solving two sudoku puzzles can be a fairly similar experience, but there's something about, say, solving a puzzle that's a list of arcade games and then solving a puzzle filled with elements from the periodic table that feels very different, even if the solving process is the same.

Of course, there's another quality that crisscrosses share with sudoku, which is that they can have quite a range of difficulty. For instance, if a grid contains only one 10-letter answer, you can write it in right away, which gets things started nice and easily. But most crisscrosses don't give you that much help. And others get particularly tricky—for instance, in a puzzle where every answer is the same length, you'll really have your work cut out for you.

The 112 puzzles in this book start out easy, and get generally harder as they go, with the trickiest ones in the back. You can start from the front and work your way through, or jump around depending on what kind of challenge you feel like having at the time. One more thing to know: Ignore spaces, punctuation, accents, and any words in parentheses (which are sometimes included for context).

Happy solving!

—Francis Heaney

MONOPOLIZING THE CONVERSATION

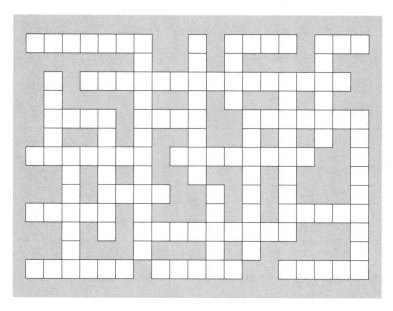

3-letter word
CAT

4-letter words
BOOT
DEED
DICE
IRON
RENT

5-letter words
CARDS
HOTEL
HOUSE
MONEY
PURSE
TITLE

6-letter words
BANKER
CANNON

7-letter words
AUCTION
READING
THIMBLE
VENTNOR
VERMONT

8-letter words
BANKRUPT
ORIENTAL
VIRGINIA

9-letter words
PARK PLACE
SHORT LINE
TENNESSEE

12-letter word
ROCKING
  HORSE

15-letter word
ELECTRIC
  COMPANY

BOWL GAME

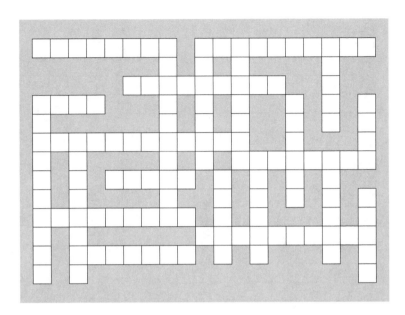

<u>4-letter words</u>
CHEX
TRIX

<u>5-letter words</u>
ALPEN
KASHI
SMORZ
TOTAL

<u>6-letter words</u>
GOLEAN
KABOOM
OREO O'S

<u>7-letter words</u>
MUESLIX
NOURISH
PUFFINS

<u>8-letter words</u>
CHEERIOS
CORN POPS
HONEY KIX

<u>9-letter words</u>
ALPHA-BITS
GRAPE-NUTS

<u>10-letter words</u>
CORN FLAKES
FROOT LOOPS
MINI-WHEATS
SMART START

<u>12-letter word</u>
RICE KRISPIES

MAKEUP TEST

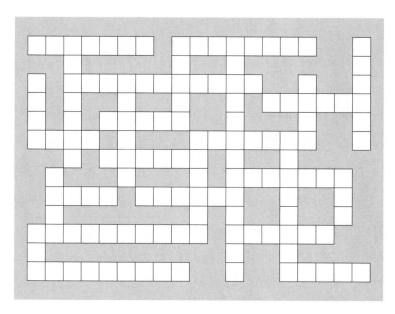

3-letter words
ELF
MAC

4-letter words
AVON
DIOR
LUSH
NARS
ULTA

5-letter words
ROUGE
MATTE
TARTE

6-letter words
BEN NYE
CHANEL
MIRROR
POMADE
PRIMER
SHADOW
SPONGE

7-letter words
BRONZER
KAT VON D
PALETTE
TOM FORD

8-letter words
EYELINER
TWEEZERS

9-letter word
CONCEALER

10-letter word
MAYBELLINE

11-letter word
MOISTURIZER

13-letter word
EYEBROW
  PENCIL

COLOR GUARD

4-letter words	6-letter words	8-letter words
FERN	CANARY	INCHWORM
GOLD	CERISE	SHAMROCK
PLUM	COPPER	TEAL BLUE
	INDIGO	
5-letter words	ORCHID	9-letter word
DENIM	SALMON	DANDELION
MAIZE	SHADOW	
MELON		10-letter words
SEPIA	7-letter words	CORNFLOWER
	FUCHSIA	FUZZY WUZZY
	SCARLET	NEON CARROT
	SUNGLOW	OUTER SPACE
	THISTLE	RAZZMATAZZ

14-letter word
WILD
   STRAWBERRY

DOUBLE DOUBLE-U

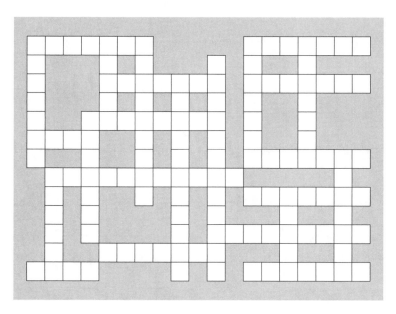

4-letter words
FWIW
WHEW

5-letter words
"WE WON!"
WOWED

6-letter word
WARSAW

7-letter words
AWKWARD
COWTOWN
DEWCLAW
NEW WAVE
SWALLOW
WAXWING
"WHAT NOW?"
WHO'S WHO
WHY WAIT
WIDOWER
WILLOWY
WOODROW
WYSIWYG

8-letter word
SNOWPLOW

9-letter words
GROW WEARY
THROW AWAY

11-letter words
WALTER WHITE
WALT WHITMAN

12-letter word
CONWAY
    TWITTY

MUSICAL ARRANGEMENT

3-letter word
ELF

4-letter words
AIDA
CATS
GIGI
MAME
NINE
RENT

5-letter words
ANNIE
CHESS
EVITA
GYPSY
ROCKY

SHREK
SMILE
TABOO

6-letter words
BARNUM
CAN-CAN
XANADU

7-letter words
CAMELOT
COMPANY
FOLLIES

8-letter words
BIG RIVER
HAMILTON
MAMMA MIA!

10-letter words
DAMES AT SEA
HELLO, DOLLY!
KISS ME, KATE
SHE LOVES ME

12-letter words
CITY OF
   ANGELS
GUYS AND
   DOLLS
SCHOOL OF
   ROCK

13-letter word
LEGALLY
   BLONDE

JAPANESE IMPORTS

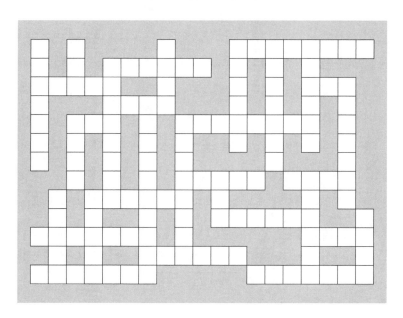

3-letter words
KOI
NOH
OBI
ZEN

4-letter words
DOJO
KOAN
KOTO
MISO
UDON
ZORI

5-letter words
MANGA
NINJA
OTAKU
SUSHI

6-letter words
BONSAI
DAIKON
HIJIKI
KIMONO
SENSEI
SHOGUN
WASABI

7-letter words
BUNRAKU
BUSHIDO
IKEBANA
JUJITSU
SATSUMA
TSUNAMI

8-letter words
KAMIKAZE
SHAMISEN
SHIBA INU
WABI SABI

10-letter word
SHABU SHABU

MALL DIRECTORY

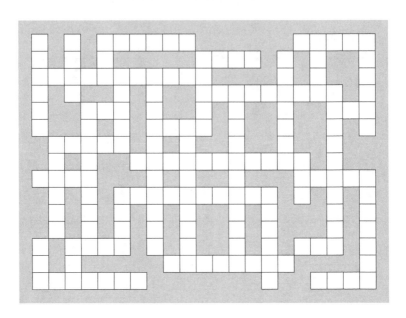

3-letter words
AMC
CVS
E.L.F.
FYE
GAP
KAY
MAC

4-letter words
ALDO
DKNY
FILA
KEDS
LIDS
SAKS
TUMI
ZARA

5-letter words
CACHE
CHLOE
FENDI
LOEWS
ZALES

6-letter words
CHAMPS
FOSSIL
SWATCH
TARGET
TJ MAXX

7-letter words
PAYLESS
SAUCONY
WET SEAL

8-letter word
JC PENNEY

9-letter words
MOLESKINE
MONTBLANC
NORDSTROM

10-letter words
LANE BRYANT
MAGGIE MOO'S

11-letter words
AUNTIE ANNE'S
KENNETH COLE
MARIE-CLAIRE
RALPH LAUREN

R2-D2

6-letter word
RUDDER

7-letter words
DARK RED
DEIRDRE
DERRIDA
MORDRED
RUDDIER
RUDYARD

8-letter words
CORRODED
SHREDDER

9-letter words
HARD BREAD
READDRESS

10-letter words
CD-ROM DRIVE
DAYDREAMER
DRIED FRUIT
FORD HYBRID
GERALD FORD
ROPE LADDER
TARDIGRADE

11-letter word
CEDAR RAPIDS

12-letter words
ARTFUL
   DODGER
PARADE
   GROUND

13-letter word
POWDERED
   SUGAR

LUCY IN THE SKY

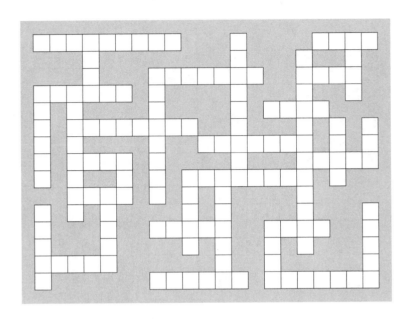

3-letter words
SKY
SUN

4-letter words
EYES
GIRL
GROW
HIGH
LUCY
OVER
PAST
PIES
TAKE
TIES

5-letter words
CALLS
DRIFT
GREEN
QUITE
THERE
TRAIN
TREES

6-letter words
ANSWER
APPEAR
BRIDGE

7-letter words
FLOWERS
SOMEONE
STATION
WAITING

8-letter words
DIAMONDS
FOUNTAIN
SUDDENLY
TOWERING

9-letter words
MARMALADE
TANGERINE

12-letter word
LOOKING
  GLASS

OZONE

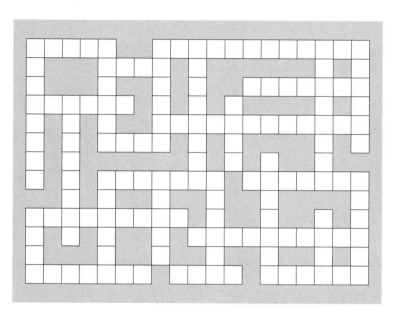

4-letter words
BOZO
DODO
GO-GO
MOOR
OSLO
YOKO

5-letter words
FRODO
HOOPS

6-letter words
BOCHCO
FORGOT
KOWTOW
NO GOOD
"NO PROB!"
OBLONG
ROCOCO
VOODOO

7-letter words
DOG DOOR
FOGHORN
MOLOTOV
PHOTO OP
ROOFTOP

8-letter words
FOLK ROCK
MOON BOOT
OFF-COLOR
WOOL MOTH

9-letter word
MOTOR POOL

10-letter word
COMMON COLD

12-letter words
BOOK OF
   MORMON
"COOL STORY,
   BRO"

SING A SONG OF SONDHEIM

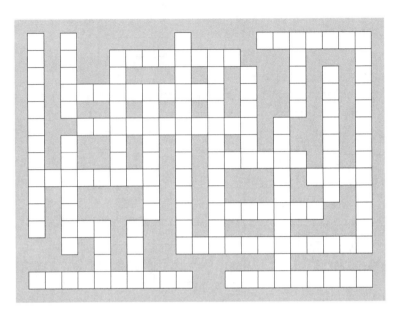

3-letter word
NOW

4-letter words
COOL
NEXT
WAIT

5-letter words
MARIA
POEMS

6-letter words
MOVE ON
SUNDAY

7-letter words
AH, PARIS!
JET SONG
OUR TIME

8-letter words
BY THE SEA
EPIPHANY
LIAISONS
LOVELAND
REMEMBER

9-letter word
ROSE'S TURN

10-letter words
IT TAKES TWO
PRETTY LADY
STAY WITH ME

11-letter word
I'M STILL HERE

12-letter words
BROADWAY
   BABY
NO ONE IS
   ALONE
THE RIGHT GIRL

13-letter words
A LITTLE PRIEST
SORRY-
   GRATEFUL

HALLOWEEN SCENE

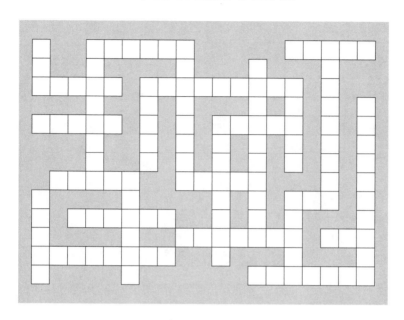

3-letter words
BAT
BOO
WIG

5-letter words
BONES
CANDY
FANGS
GHOST
GHOUL
MUMMY
SKULL
TREAT
TRICK
WITCH

6-letter words
COBWEB
POTION
SPIDER

7-letter words
COSTUME
PUMPKIN

8-letter words
BLACK CAT
CAULDRON
CEMETERY
GRUESOME

9-letter words
MOONLIGHT
SCARECROW

10-letter words
BROOMSTICK
GRAVESTONE

WHAT'S THE DEAL?

3-letter words
GIN
MAO
WAR

4-letter words
GOLF
SKAT
SPIT

5-letter words
CINCH
OMAHA
PITCH
POKER
RUMMY

6-letter words
BRIDGE
CASINO
HAVANA
OH HELL
SPADES
SPOONS

7-letter words
CANASTA
ELEUSIS
HIGH-LOW
PYRAMID

8-letter words
CANFIELD
FREECELL
I DOUBT IT
KLONDIKE
PINOCHLE
SCORPION
WEREWOLF

THEY'VE GOT THEIR UPS & DOWNS

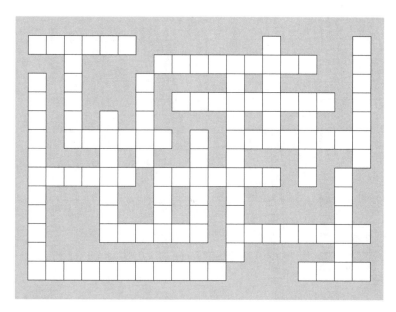

4-letter words
FROG
YO-YO

5-letter words
CRANE
HI-HAT

6-letter words
GEYSER
MELODY
PISTON
PRICES
RABBIT
SEESAW
TIGGER
ZIPPER

7-letter words
DEFICIT
EYEBROW
FLY BALL

8-letter words
ELEVATOR
KANGAROO

9-letter words
BIRD'S WING
POGO STICK

11-letter words
MODEL ROCKET
STOCK MARKET
TEMPERATURE

A PUZZLING PUZZLE

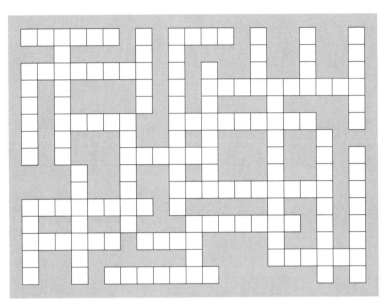

4-letter words
BURR
CAVE
LITS
MAZE
TAPA

5-letter words
HASHI
MASYU
REBUS

6-letter words
IQ TEST
JIGSAW
KAKURO
KENKEN
SPIRAL
TRIVIA

7-letter words
ANAGRAM
CRYPTIC
END VIEW
SHIKAKU

8-letter words
ACROSTIC
DOT-TO-DOT
HEYAWAKE
NONOGRAM
TANGRAMS

9-letter words
ODD MAN OUT
WHODUNITS

10-letter words
CRISSCROSS
ESCAPE ROOM

11-letter words
MINESWEEPER
SLITHERLINK

SHIPSHAPE

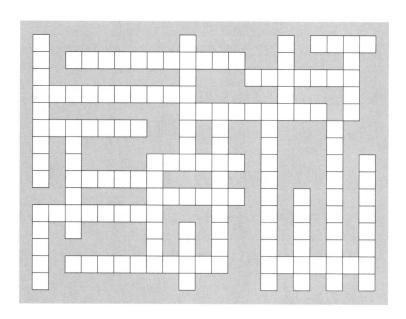

4-letter words
ARGO
ORCA

5-letter words
CAINE
MAINE
PINTA

6-letter words
BOUNTY
MINNOW
NIMITZ
YAMATO

7-letter words
CALYPSO
KON-TIKI
MONITOR
TITANIC
VICTORY

8-letter words
BISMARCK
MISSOURI
POTEMKIN

9-letter words
ENDEAVOUR
MERRIMACK

10-letter words
ENTERPRISE
GOLDEN HIND
JOLLY ROGER
RED OCTOBER

11-letter words
ANDREA DORIA
MARY CELESTE

GIVE ME A SIGN

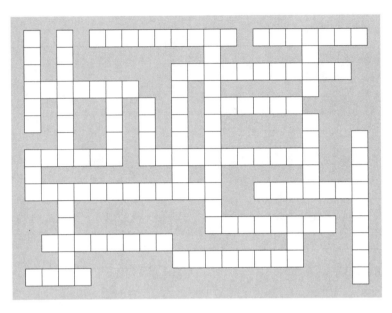

3-letter words
DIP
ICY

4-letter words
BUMP
HILL
SLOW

5-letter words
RADAR
YIELD

6-letter words
DETOUR
GRAVEL
SCHOOL
TUNNEL

7-letter words
BUS STOP
DEAD END
NO U-TURN

8-letter words
DEER XING
NO OUTLET
REST AREA
WORK ZONE
WRONG WAY

9-letter words
BRIDGE OUT
MERGE LEFT

11-letter words
PARK AND RIDE
ROAD
  NARROWS

12-letter words
FLAGGER
  AHEAD
PASS WITH
  CARE

EARN YOUR STRIPES

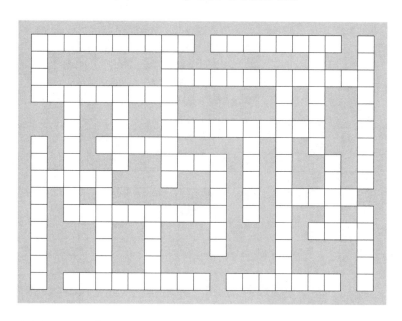

4-letter words
BASS
KUDU
SOCK

5-letter words
NYALA
OKAPI
SKUNK
STRAW
TIGER
WALDO
ZEBRA

6-letter words
SAMOAS
U.S. FLAG

7-letter words
IBM LOGO
RACECAR
REFEREE

8-letter words
JAILBIRD
NINE BALL

9-letter words
BUMBLEBEE
CLOWNFISH
CROSSWALK
LAYER CAKE
SANDSTONE

10-letter words
BARBER POLE
CORAL SNAKE
LEMUR'S TAIL

13-letter words
NO-PASSING
  ZONE
YANKEE
  UNIFORM

TRAFFIC JAM

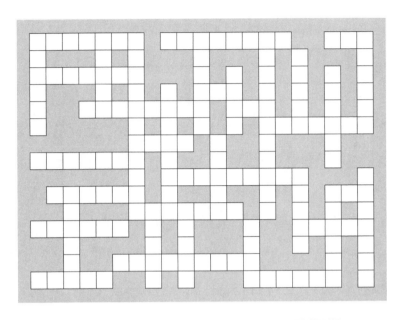

3-letter words
GTO
LTD
VUE
XKE

4-letter words
DART
NEON
VOLT

5-letter words
ARIES
CRUZE
EDSEL
E-TYPE
FOCUS

IROC-Z
JETTA
PINTO

6-letter words
ACCORD
DENALI
ESCORT
ESPRIT
LEGEND
RANGER
SPRITE
TIGUAN
VEYRON

7-letter words
AIRFLOW
BERETTA

ELEMENT
MUSTANG
RAINIER
SKYLARK

8-letter words
CORVETTE
ESCALADE
WAGONEER

9-letter words
ECONOLINE
PT CRUISER

11-letter words
KARMANN GHIA
THUNDERBIRD

EAT UP!

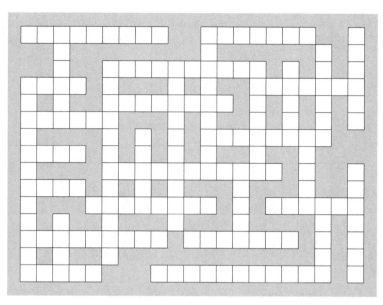

4-letter words
FLAN
HASH
NAAN
ZITI

5-letter words
ADOBO
BLINI
CHAAT
CREPE
GUMBO
RAITA

6-letter words
DIM SUM
KISHKE
QUICHE
SAMOSA
SCAMPI

7-letter words
CHOLENT
EGG ROLL
GOULASH
PIEROGI
RISOTTO

8-letter words
ALOO GOBI
CHILI DOG
MEAT LOAF

9-letter words
CARBONARA
FRICASSEE
KIDNEY PIE

10-letter words
MINESTRONE
SHISH KABOB

11-letter words
CHANA MASALA
RATATOUILLE

12-letter words
HASENPFEFFER
MAC AND
   CHEESE

BACK AND FORTH

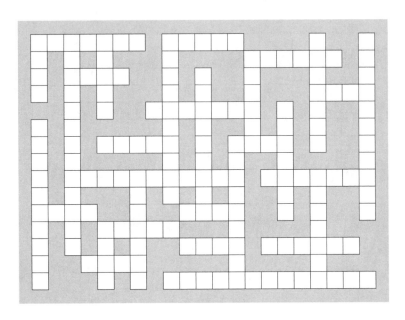

4-letter words
ABBA
DEED
EMME
KOOK
MA'AM
NOON
OTTO
PEEP
TOOT

5-letter words
KAYAK
MY GYM
NOT ON
SHAHS

6-letter words
HANNAH
TOP POT
TUT-TUT

7-letter words
A TOYOTA
DON'T NOD
PA'S A SAP
ROTATOR
TIKI KIT
TUNA NUT
UFO TOFU

9-letter words
EVIL OLIVE
OH, NO! DON
    HO!

10-letter words
DOG SEES GOD
"NAOMI," I
    MOAN

11-letter words
MADAM, I'M
    ADAM
NEIL, AN ALIEN

13-letter words
SO MANY
    DYNAMOS
WONTONS?
    NOT NOW

IN THE SWIM

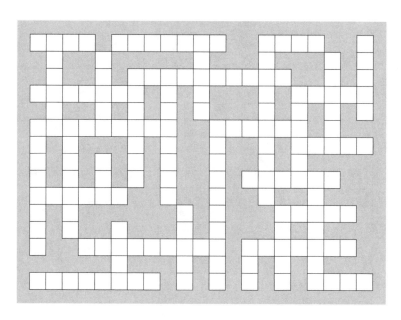

3-letter words
COD
GAR

4-letter words
GOBY
HAKE
OPAH
SHAD

5-letter words
GUPPY
MORAY
SHARK
SKATE
SMELT
SPRAT
TETRA
TROUT

6-letter words
DARTER
DORADO
MINNOW
MUSSEL
PLAICE
SALMON

7-letter words
GROUPER
HALIBUT
LAMPREY
OCTOPUS
SEA BASS
TILAPIA

8-letter words
JOHN DORY
MENHADEN
STURGEON

9-letter words
GRASS CARP
JELLYFISH

10-letter words
GIANT SQUID
HAMMERHEAD
MUDSKIPPER

IT'S TIME TO MEET THE MUPPETS

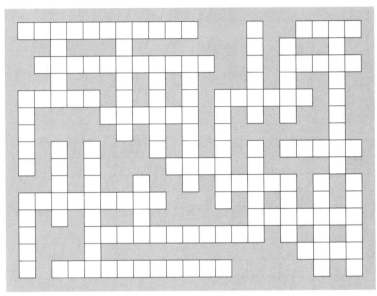

4-letter words
BERT
BOBO
ELMO
PEPE
ZOOT

5-letter words
COUNT
ERNIE
FLOYD
GONZO
MOKEY
OSCAR
ROBIN
WANDA
WAYNE

6-letter words
ANIMAL
BEAKER
FOZZIE
JANICE
KERMIT
SLIMEY
WALTER

7-letter words
CAMILLA
SCOOTER
STATLER

8-letter words
BETTY LOU
DON MUSIC

9-letter words
BEAN BUNNY
GUY SMILEY

11-letter words
ABBY CADABBY
MARVIN SUGGS
SAM THE EAGLE
UNCLE DEADLY

EXCLAMATION STATION

4-letter words
ALAS
AMEN
GOSH
SHOO
TA-DA
UH-OH
WHEE
WHEW
WHOA
YUCK

5-letter words
ADIEU
EGADS
PSHAW
SALUD
SKOAL
YAHOO
YIKES

6-letter words
BANZAI
ENCORE
EUREKA
LA-DI-DA
PIP-PIP
PRESTO
RIGHTO
YIPPEE

7-letter words
HEADS UP
JEEPERS
MY STARS
NAMASTE
OOH-LA-LA
WHOOPEE
WOE IS ME

8-letter words
HARRUMPH
MEA CULPA

10-letter words
HOT DIGGITY
WOWIE ZOWIE

DIZZY WITH DISNEY

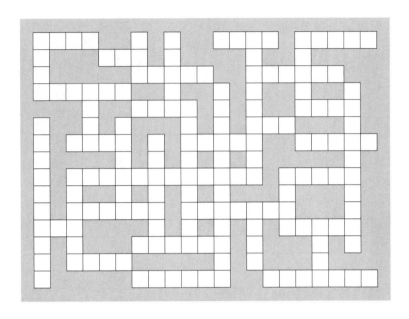

3-letter words
ABU
DOC
KAA
PUA

4-letter words
ANNA
ELSA
FLIT
JANE
NALA
OLAF
SCAR
SMEE
SVEN
TERK
YZMA

5-letter words
ALICE
ARIEL
GENIE
GOOFY
KANGA
MOANA
TIANA
WENDY

6-letter words
AURORA
EEYORE
MEGARA
MERLIN
NAVEEN
SHENZI
URSULA

7-letter words
JASMINE
LUCIFER
TAMATOA

9-letter words
ALAN-A-DALE
ESMERALDA

10-letter words
MAID MARIAN
MISS BIANCA

12-letter words
ICHABOD
  CRANE
UNCLE
  SCROOGE

DIZZIER WITH DISNEY

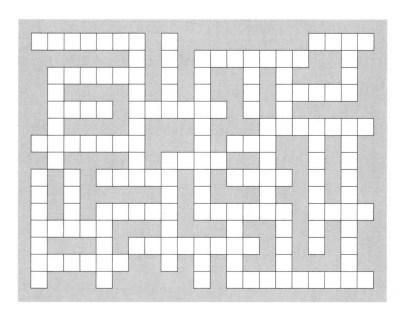

3-letter words
OWL
ROO

4-letter words
CLEO
HUEY
IAGO
JOCK
LILO
NANA
ZAZU
ZERO

5-letter words
BAMBI
BASIL
BEAST
BELLE
CHI-FU
LOUIE
MEEKO
SIMBA
TIMON

6-letter words
MOWGLI
MR. TOAD
OSWALD
RABBIT
TANTOR
TIGGER

7-letter words
BERLIOZ
DUCHESS
LUMIERE
MAURICE
MAXIMUS
MONSTRO

8-letter words
DORMOUSE
RAPUNZEL

9-letter words
LAUNCHPAD
STROMBOLI

10-letter words
CINDERELLA
DR. FACILIER

WE'RE FROM FRANCE

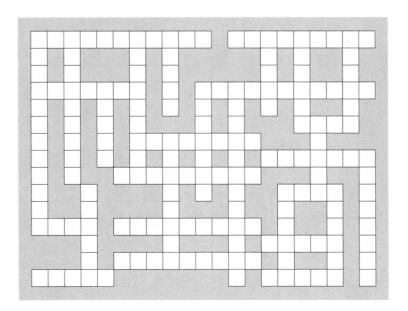

4-letter words
ÉLAN
ÉPÉE
ROUÉ

5-letter words
DECOR
ETUDE
FORTE
MELEE
OUTRÉ
SAUTÉ
VOILÀ

6-letter words
AUTEUR
BON MOT
ÉCLAIR
ENCORE
ENTRÉE

7-letter words
HABITUÉ
IMPASSE
MONTAGE

8-letter words
EN POINTE
ESCARGOT
PEIGNOIR

9-letter words
DÉCOLLETÉ
DE RIGUEUR
ENTRE NOUS
GRENADIER
NONPAREIL
TÊTE-À-TÊTE

11-letter words
CONTRETEMPS
HORS
    D'OEUVRE

12-letter words
CHAISE
    LONGUE
RESTAURATEUR

SAY "CHEESE"

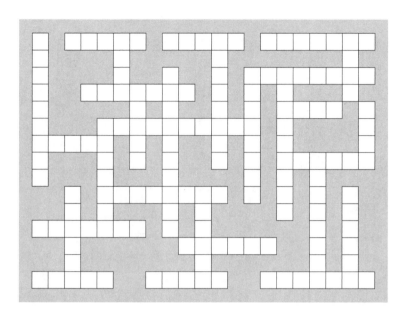

4-letter words
BLEU
BRIE
EDAM
FETA

5-letter words
ANEJO
BANON
BRICK
COLBY
DERBY
GOUDA

6-letter words
ASIAGO
CHEVRE
COTIJA
PANEER
TILSIT

7-letter words
CHEDDAR
GJETOST
LANGRES
RICOTTA
SAPSAGO

8-letter words
AMERICAN
CHESHIRE
PARMESAN
PECORINO
TALEGGIO

9-letter words
LIMBURGER
REBLOCHON

10-letter words
LANCASHIRE
STRACCHINO

ARCADIA

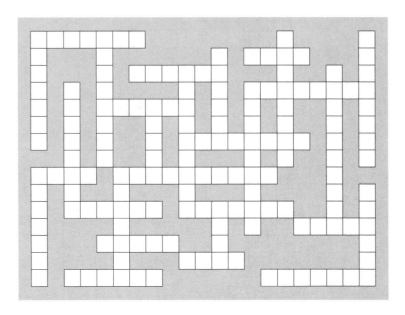

4-letter words
GORF
MR. DO
PONG
TRON

5-letter words
JOUST
PENGO
Q*BERT

6-letter words
CONTRA
NBA JAM
OUTRUN
TEKKEN
TETRIS
ZAXXON

7-letter words
BERZERK
PHOENIX
RAMPAGE
REACTOR
TEMPEST
XEVIOUS

8-letter words
ARKANOID
BREAKOUT
COMMANDO
PAPERBOY
PUNCH-OUT!!
STARGATE

9-letter words
SPY HUNTER
TIME PILOT

10-letter words
BATTLEZONE
DARK ESCAPE

COMPOSE YOURSELF

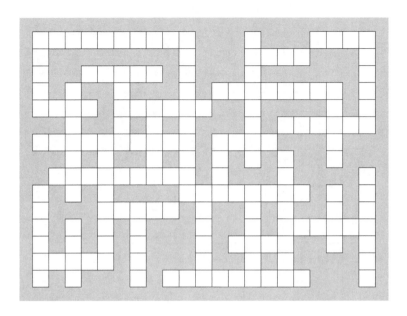

4-letter words
BACH
BERG
CAGE
IVES
LANG
MONK
PÄRT
SHAW

5-letter words
ADAMS
GRIEG
HOLST
LEHAR
LISZT

REICH
SATIE
VERDI

6-letter words
CHOPIN
DELIUS
DVOŘÁK
GLINKA
LIGETI
MOZART
TALLIS

7-letter words
BERLIOZ
JANÁČEK

8-letter words
BRUCKNER
HONEGGER
SCHUBERT
SCHUMANN
SIBELIUS

9-letter words
GINASTERA
VON BINGEN

10-letter words
PALESTRINA
SAINT-SAËNS
VILLA-LOBOS

HOT STUFF

3-letter words
AIR
DOG
TIP
TUB

4-letter words
CAKE
COMB
LAVA
MEAL
SEAT
SPOT
TAKE
WIRE
YOGA
ZONE

5-letter words
COALS
COCOA
FLASH
FUDGE
LUNCH
PANTS
PLATE
SAUCE

6-letter words
BUTTON
CEREAL
COFFEE
PEPPER
POTATO
TAMALE
WHEELS

7-letter words
MUSTARD
PRETZEL

9-letter words
CHOCOLATE
CROSS BUNS

MAGAZINE RACK

HOLIDAYS FROM ALL OVER

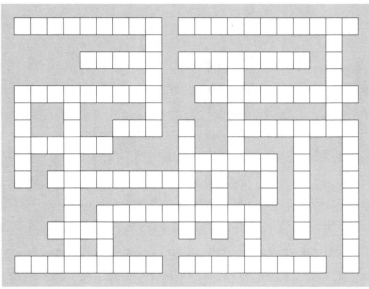

3-letter words
BON
TET

4-letter words
HOLI
LENT
YULE

5-letter words
PURIM
VESAK

6-letter words
ADVENT
DIWALI
MAY DAY

7-letter words
BELTANE
DUSSERA
KWANZAA
RAMADAN
SAMHAIN

8-letter words
ARBOR DAY
LAG B'OMER

9-letter words
CANDLEMAS
CHRISTMAS
HALLOWEEN
MAGHA PUJA
MARDI GRAS
YOM KIPPUR

10-letter words
GOLDEN WEEK
LUGHNASADH

11-letter words
HANA MATSURI
WHITSUNTIDE

LOOK! UP IN THE SKY!

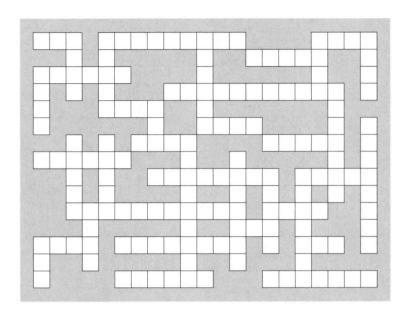

3-letter words
AUK
KEA
OWL
SUN
UFO

4-letter words
DUCK
GNAT
HAWK
KITE
MARS
MOON
MOTH
STAR
SWAN
TERN
WASP

5-letter words
ANGEL
BLIMP
CLOUD
DUMBO
EAGLE
GOOSE
SMOKE

6-letter words
FALCON
ICARUS
METEOR
OSPREY

7-letter words
BALLOON
ECLIPSE
SEAGULL
SWALLOW

8-letter words
AIRPLANE
MOSQUITO
SUPERMAN

9-letter words
CONTRAILS
PARACHUTE

11-letter words
MARY POPPINS
PTERODACTYL

EPIC FAIL

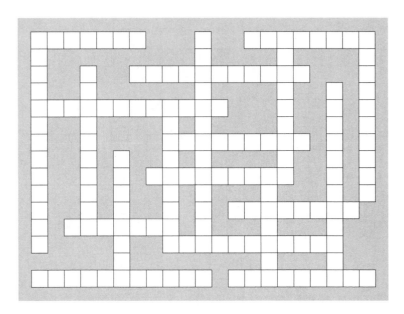

7-letter words
AFAR OFF
FEIFFER
LIFTOFF

8-letter words
FILM BUFF
IFFY WI-FI
RIFFRAFF

9-letter words
FISTICUFF
JEFF FAHEY
KERFUFFLE
LUFTWAFFE
TUFF ENUFF

10-letter words
"FEE FI FO FUM"
STEFFI GRAF

11-letter words
FALL AFOUL OF
FORMAL OFFER
FROZEN STIFF

12-letter words
CHIEF OF
   STAFF
FIRTH OF
   FORTH

13-letter words
DREYFUS
   AFFAIR
FRENCH
   MASTIFF

FLATLAND

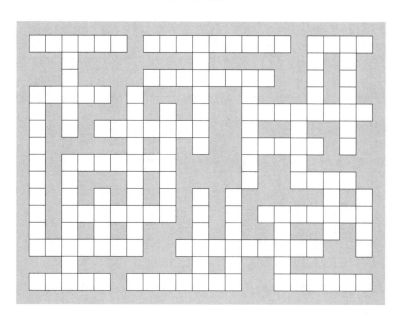

4-letter words
CAPE
FELT
LEAF
RAFT
TILE

5-letter words
CREPE
FUTON
PAPER
SCARF
SHEET
TOWEL

6-letter words
CARPET
CD CASE
FOLDER
PANINI
TABLET

7-letter words
BAND-AID
COASTER
NAMETAG
PALETTE
PANCAKE
PLACARD
PLYWOOD
POP-TART
RECEIPT
T-SQUARE

8-letter words
MAGAZINE
MOUSE PAD
PAMPHLET

9-letter words
BILLBOARD
BIRCH BARK

10-letter words
PHOTO STRIP
WINDOWPANE

PITCH PERFECT

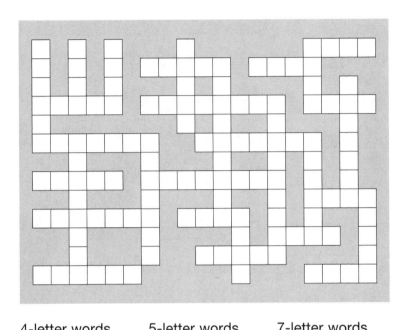

4-letter words
BLUE
CONE
DEAN
FORD
HOYT
KAAT
ODOM
RYAN
WEBB
WYNN
ZITO

5-letter words
BROWN
GAGNE
SPAHN
TIANT
VIOLA
YOUNG

6-letter words
DRABEK
GUIDRY
NIEKRO

7-letter words
BUEHRLE
CARLTON
KERSHAW
MUSSINA
WADDELL

8-letter words
DRYSDALE
LINCECUM
RIGHETTI

9-letter words
ALEXANDER
MATHEWSON

RHYME TIME

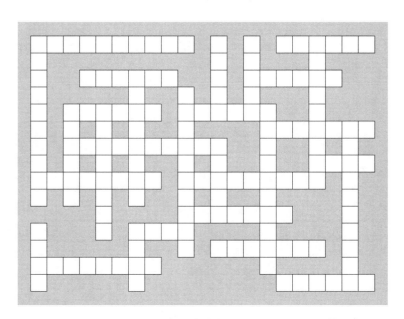

4-letter words
FUBU
HOBO
HULU
NO-GO

5-letter words
GOPRO
SCI-FI
SEE ME

6-letter words
BAR CAR
FAT CAT
HOBNOB
HOT POT
ONE TON
PICNIC
TEX-MEX

7-letter words
CHIP DIP
ILL WILL
SKY-HIGH

8-letter words
BOOB TUBE
CHOP SHOP
COOKBOOK
TRUE-BLUE

9-letter words
PRIME TIME
RHINE WINE

10-letter words
BLUE'S CLUES
CHEAT SHEET
CHICK FLICK
HOCUS POCUS
LEGAL EAGLE
NIGHT LIGHT

SCHOOL SPIRIT

3-letter words
COE
MIT

4-letter words
DUKE
ELON
PACE
REED
RICE
UCLA
YALE

5-letter words
PRATT
TUFTS

6-letter words
BAYLOR
ITHACA
MCGILL
POMONA
PURDUE
TULANE

7-letter words
ADELPHI
AMHERST
ANTIOCH
CLEMSON
FORDHAM
GONZAGA
HOFSTRA
LASALLE
RUTGERS

8-letter words
BRANDEIS
COLUMBIA
WESLEYAN

9-letter words
NOTRE DAME
SETON HALL

10-letter words
BENNINGTON
SWARTHMORE

MEASURING UP

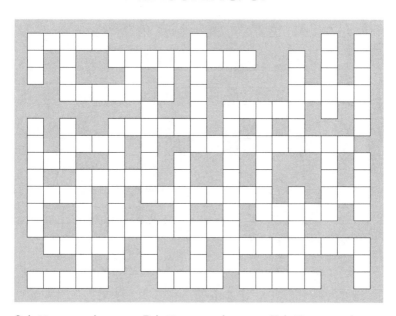

3-letter words
CUP
DAY
EON
ERG
OHM
RAD
ROD
TON

4-letter words
ACRE
BOLT
GILL
PICA
PINT
REAM

5-letter words
CABLE
CARAT
CHAIN
CUBIT
FIFTH
GAUSS
GRAIN
HENRY
LUMEN
MINIM
QUART
TESLA

6-letter words
DECADE
FATHOM
MICRON
OCTANT
PASCAL

7-letter words
CALIBER
FURLONG
SCRUPLE
SIEMENS

8-letter words
ROENTGEN
TEASPOON

9-letter words
CUBIC YARD
FORTNIGHT
MEGAHERTZ

10-letter words
FLUID OUNCE
SQUARE MILE

TOO WISE

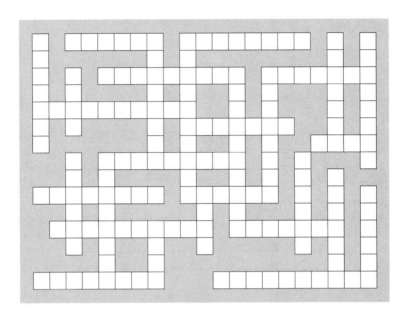

4-letter words
"MY, MY"
SKYY
SYFY
YO-YO

6-letter words
MAYFLY
SAY YES
SYDNEY
WAYLAY
YEARLY

7-letter words
CRYBABY
DYNASTY
LAZY EYE
MYSTERY
ROYALTY
WYSIWYG

8-letter words
DERBY DAY
KAY KYSER
LUYENDYK
MYRNA LOY
RICKY JAY
SYMPATHY
"WHY WORRY?"

9-letter words
ETYMOLOGY
WAVY GRAVY

10-letter words
ALLY SHEEDY
BLOODY MARY
MILEY CYRUS
WAYNE BRADY
YUL BRYNNER

TEAMWORK

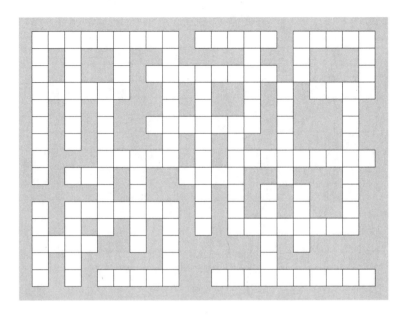

3-letter words
SKY
SUN

4-letter words
HEAT
JETS
METS
NETS
RAMS
WILD

5-letter words
BILLS
COLTS
HAWKS
SPURS

STORM
TWINS
WINGS

6-letter words
ANGELS
DYNAMO
GALAXY
IMPACT
RAPIDS

7-letter words
BENGALS
MERCURY
RANGERS
RAPTORS

8-letter words
RED BULLS
SENATORS
STEELERS

9-letter words
CARDINALS
CAVALIERS
LIGHTNING
MAVERICKS
PREDATORS

10-letter words
BUCCANEERS
REVOLUTION

IT'S ELEMENTARY

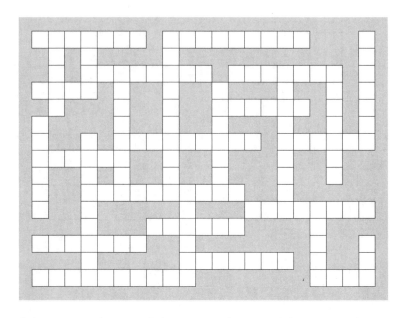

3-letter word
TIN

4-letter words
GOLD
LEAD
NEON

5-letter words
ARGON
RADON

6-letter words
COBALT
INDIUM
IODINE
NICKEL
OSMIUM
SODIUM

7-letter words
DUBNIUM
GALLIUM
KRYPTON
NIOBIUM
SILICON
THORIUM
URANIUM

8-letter words
ANTIMONY
SAMARIUM
TUNGSTEN

9-letter words
LANTHANUM
PLUTONIUM
POTASSIUM
STRONTIUM

10-letter words
PHOSPHORUS
PROMETHIUM
TENNESSINE

TOM, DICK, AND HARRY

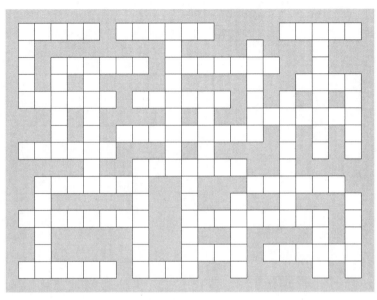

4-letter words
KITE
LIME
REID
YORK

5-letter words
BRADY
CARAY
CLARK
DELAY
GREEN
THUMB
TRACY

6-letter words
BOSLEY
BUTTON
CLANCY
ENBERG
HAMLIN
LEHRER
MORGAN
PARTCH
POSTON
POTTER
SEAVER

7-letter words
DASCHLE
EBERSOL
HOUDINI
NILSSON
VAN DYKE
VILSACK

8-letter words
ANDERSON
BERGERON
SMOTHERS
STOPPARD

9-letter words
COURTENAY
DASTARDLY
VAN PATTEN

THAT'S SUPER

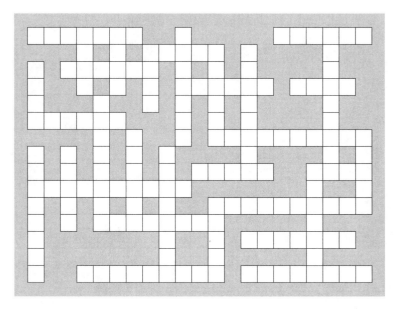

<u>4-letter words</u>
ATOM
BANE
DRAX
LOKI
PYRO
WASP

<u>5-letter words</u>
ANGEL
BEAST
BLADE
GROOT
JOKER

<u>6-letter words</u>
ANARKY
FALCON
GAMORA
ICEMAN
KRYPTO
THANOS

<u>7-letter words</u>
PENGUIN
SANDMAN
SHE-HULK
ZATANNA

<u>8-letter words</u>
BRAINIAC
DEADSHOT
GALACTUS
LUKE CAGE
SINESTRO
SUPERBOY

<u>9-letter words</u>
LEX LUTHOR
POISON IVY

<u>10-letter words</u>
JUGGERNAUT
PLASTIC MAN
SWAMP THING

RAINING CATS AND DOGS

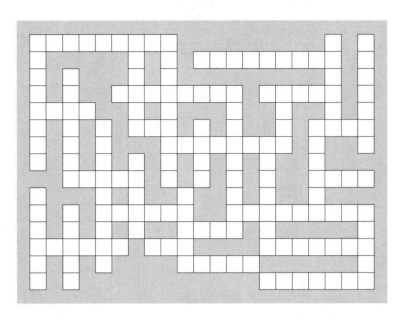

3-letter words
EEK
REN

4-letter words
BOLT
CUJO
MILO
NANA
ODIE
RUFF

5-letter words
ASTRO
BALTO
MOCHI
PONGO
RUFUS
SIMBA
SOCKS

6-letter words
ARLENE
AZRAEL
FIGARO
NERMAL
PEPITA
TIGGER

7-letter words
FELICIA
MCGRUFF
SCAT CAT
SI AND AM
TOONCES

8-letter words
SGT. TIBBS
SNOWBELL
TOULOUSE

9-letter words
MARMADUKE
OLD YELLER
RIN TIN TIN
SCOOBY-DOO
SYLVESTER
WHITE FANG

CAPITALIZED

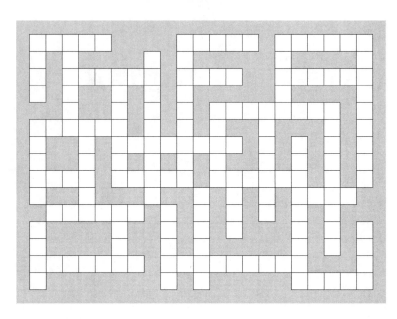

4-letter words
APIA
BERN
DILI
DOHA
JUBA
KIEV
OSLO
SUVA

5-letter words
ABUJA
ACCRA
DAKAR
KABUL

MINSK
PARIS
SOFIA
TUNIS

6-letter words
ASTANA
BANJUL
LUANDA
MALABO
MANAMA
NASSAU
NIAMEY
ROSEAU
TEHRAN

7-letter words
ALGIERS
BAGHDAD
ST. JOHN'S

8-letter words
DAMASCUS
HELSINKI

9-letter words
JAMESTOWN
LJUBLJANA
NAYPYIDAW
NUKU'ALOFA
PODGORICA
ST. GEORGE'S

RR CROSSING

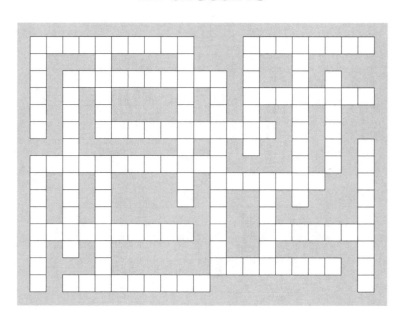

6-letter words
RAG RUG
RAH-RAH
RATED R
ROB ROY

7-letter words
RAN RIOT
REC ROOM
RED RAIN

8-letter words
RENT ROLL
RIB ROAST
RING ROAD
RIVER RAT
ROD RODDY

9-letter words
RAY ROMANO
RETRO ROCK

10-letter words
RANGER RICK
RATSO RIZZO
RITA RUDNER
ROTO-ROOTER
RUSTED ROOT

11-letter words
RAW RECRUITS
ROGER RABBIT

12-letter words
RABBLE-
   ROUSER
RICH RELATIVE

FOR VEGETARIANS

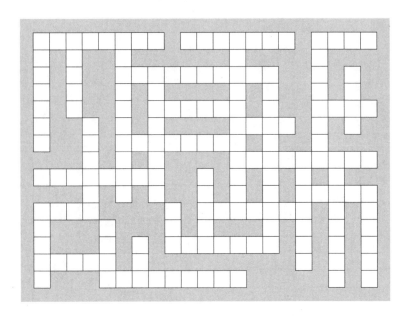

3-letter words
PEA
YAM

4-letter words
BEET
CORN
DILL
KALE
LEEK
OKRA

5-letter words
ANCHO
CHARD
MOREL
OLIVE
ONION

6-letter words
JICAMA
LENTIL
SESAME

7-letter words
ARUGULA
AVOCADO
CASSAVA
CHAYOTE
ROMAINE

8-letter words
CHICKPEA
CUCUMBER
GARBANZO
JALAPEÑO
MUSHROOM
PURSLANE

9-letter words
ASPARAGUS
TOMATILLO

10-letter words
BELL PEPPER
LEMONGRASS

11-letter words
GRAPE LEAVES
SWEET POTATO

LAUGHING MATTERS

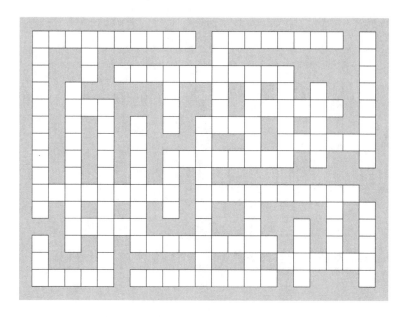

3-letter words
ALF
FLO
MOM

4-letter words
M*A*S*H
SOAP
TAXI
VEEP

5-letter words
COACH
ELLEN
MAUDE
(The) NANNY
WINGS

6-letter words
BECKER
BENSON
F TROOP
GIDGET
MOESHA
(The) OFFICE
SCRUBS

8-letter words
GET SMART
MISTER ED
(The) MUNSTERS
ROSEANNE

9-letter words
BROAD CITY
ENTOURAGE
MY TWO DADS

10-letter words
COUGAR TOWN
FAMILY TIES
(The) JEFFERSONS
TENACIOUS D

11-letter words
(The) FACTS OF
    LIFE
JUST SHOOT ME
WHO'S THE
    BOSS?

LET'S DANCE

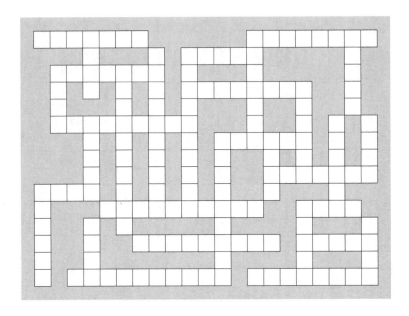

4-letter words
BUMP
CLOG
FRUG
HORA
MOSH
POGO
REEL
WHIP

5-letter words
LIMBO
MAMBO
RUMBA
TANGO
VOGUE

6-letter words
CANCAN
HUSTLE
NAE NAE
PAVANE

7-letter words
BOURRÉE
HOEDOWN
ONE-STEP
SHUFFLE

8-letter words
HABANERA
HAND JIVE
RIGADOON

9-letter words
COTILLION
POLONAISE
QUADRILLE

10-letter words
CHARLESTON
RUNNING MAN
SEGUIDILLA
TARANTELLA
TURKEY TROT

TRIAL RUN

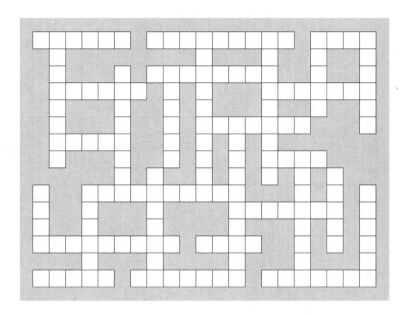

4-letter words
CASE
JURY
SUIT
TORT

5-letter words
BENCH
CLERK
CRIME
GAVEL

6-letter words
ACQUIT
DECREE
EXPERT
FRAMED
MOTIVE
RECESS

7-letter words
ADJOURN
ALLEGED
FOREMAN
GAG RULE
HEARING
PRO BONO

8-letter words
ARGUMENT
CLEMENCY
EVIDENCE
REBUTTAL

9-letter words
NOT GUILTY
PRECEDENT
YOUR HONOR

10-letter words
ACCUSATION
COURTHOUSE
DUE PROCESS

INTERIOR DECORATING

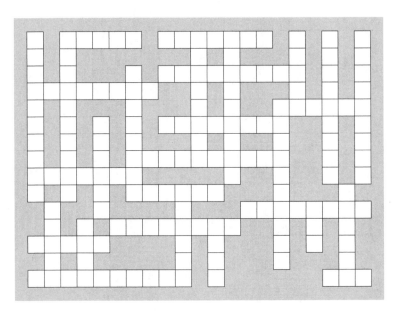

3-letter words
BED
RUG

4-letter words
POUF
SOFA

5-letter words
CHAIR
COUCH
FUTON
HUTCH

6-letter words
BUREAU
CHAISE
ROCKER
SCONCE
TV TRAY

7-letter words
ÉTAGÈRE
TALLBOY

8-letter words
BASSINET
BOOKCASE
COATRACK
CREDENZA
LOVE SEAT
ROLLAWAY

9-letter words
BANQUETTE
DAVENPORT
INGLENOOK
SECTIONAL

10-letter words
CANDELABRA
CEILING FAN
CHIFFONIER
FOUR-POSTER
NIGHTSTAND

MATH APPEAL

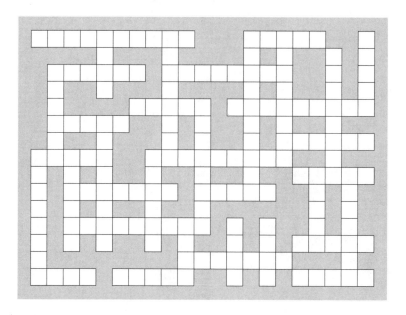

4-letter words
AREA
AXIS
LINE
MEAN
ROOT

5-letter words
ACUTE
CURVE
DIGIT
GRAPH
LIMIT
PLANE
POINT

PRISM
PROOF
RATIO
TORUS

6-letter words
CONVEX
OBLONG
OBTUSE
SCALAR
SPHERE

7-letter words
ORDINAL
PRODUCT
TANGENT

8-letter words
ABSCISSA
ADDITION
INFINITY
MULTIPLY
PARABOLA
PARALLEL
SINUSOID

9-letter words
CARTESIAN
POSTULATE
SET THEORY

10-letter words
PROPORTION
PYTHAGORAS

FLOWER POWER

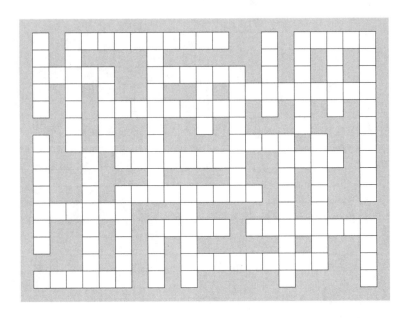

4-letter words
ARUM
DILL
IRIS
PLUM
ROSE

5-letter words
CAPER
HOSTA
LILAC
LOTUS
PANSY
POPPY
SEDUM

6-letter words
ALLIUM
AZALEA
COSMOS
LUPINE
SALVIA
ZINNIA

7-letter words
BEE BALM
PETUNIA

8-letter words
CLEMATIS
CYCLAMEN
MAGNOLIA
MANDRAKE
SWEET PEA

9-letter words
ARTEMISIA
DANDELION
EDELWEISS
NARCISSUS
SUNFLOWER

10-letter words
PINCUSHION
RUE ANEMONE
SNAPDRAGON

A TRIP TO THE HARDWARE STORE

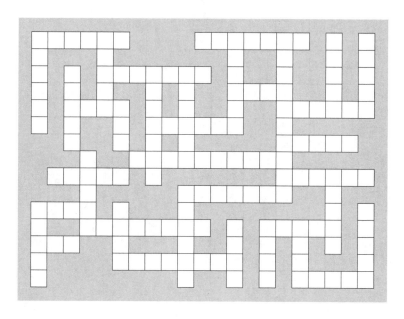

3-letter words
AWL
PVC

4-letter words
HASP
NAIL
PIPE
RAKE
TAPE
TARP
WOOD

5-letter words
AUGER
BEVEL
BRACE
HINGE

LATCH
LATHE
O-RING
PLANE
REBAR
RIVET
SCREW
VALVE

6-letter words
C-CLAMP
EYELET
PLIERS
PULLEY
ROUTER
SQUARE
TROWEL
WELDER

7-letter words
AIR HOSE
BRACKET
CONDUIT
CROWBAR

8-letter words
DUST MASK
TOOL BELT

10-letter words
SAFETY VEST
X-ACTO KNIFE

MR. AND MRS.

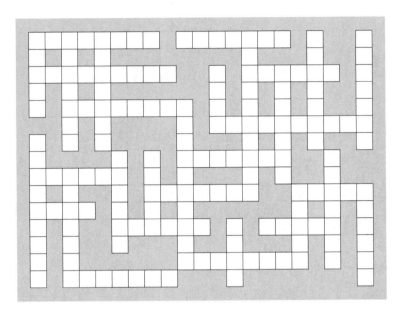

4-letter words
BILL
DASH
SHOW

5-letter words
BOFFO
BRADY
BURNS
RIGHT
SLATE

6-letter words
KOTTER
LIMPET
ROARKE
ROBOTO
SOFFEL

7-letter words
ARKADIN
BASSMAN
BEASLEY
GOODBAR
MCTHING
MINIVER
NICE GUY
NORRELL
PEACOCK
PEEPERS
SANDMAN

8-letter words
BASEBALL
DALLOWAY
MALAPROP

9-letter words
FANTASTIC
WORLDWIDE

10-letter words
OLLIVANDER
POTATO HEAD
WEATHERBEE

CALIFORNIA, HERE WE COME

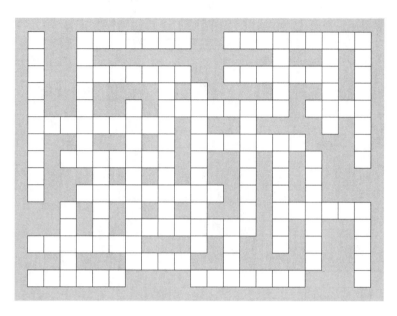

4-letter words
BREA
LODI
NAPA

5-letter words
CHICO
INDIO
RIPON

6-letter words
CLOVIS
LOMPOC
LOOMIS
OXNARD

7-letter words
ALAMEDA
ANAHEIM
BELMONT
COMPTON
MODESTO
NEEDLES
NORWALK
SAN JOSE
SOLVANG

8-letter words
PASADENA
SAN MATEO
STOCKTON
TEMECULA
TORRANCE

9-letter words
CLAREMONT
COSTA MESA
MONTCLAIR

10-letter words
LOS ANGELES
SANTA CLARA
SEBASTOPOL
YORBA LINDA

CLEAN UP YOUR ACT

3-letter words
ALL
BIZ
ERA
FAB
JOY

4-letter words
AJAX
DIAL
DOVE
ECOS
LAVA
LUSH
OLAY
PERT
T/GEL

TIDE
XTRA

5-letter words
BORAX
CHEER
COAST
DREFT
IVORY
LEVER
PEARS
PRELL
PUREX
SUAVE

6-letter words
AUSSIE
AVEENO

CARESS
ECOVER
KIEHL'S
NEXXUS
PERSIL

7-letter words
CASCADE
SUNSILK

8-letter words
LIFEBUOY
OXICLEAN
SOFTSOAP

9-letter words
L'OCCITANE
SAFEGUARD

HAIR THERE AND EVERYWHERE

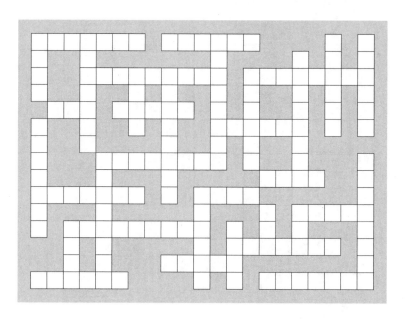

3-letter words
BOB
BUN
WIG

4-letter words
AFRO
CONK
FADE
PERM
POUF
UPDO

5-letter words
BANGS
BRAID
BUTCH

6-letter words
CAESAR
DREADS
MARCEL
MOPTOP
MULLET
ODANGO
POODLE

7-letter words
BEEHIVE
CHIGNON
CREW CUT
FLAT-TOP
PAGEBOY
TOPKNOT

8-letter words
COMBOVER
CORNROWS
DIDO FLIP
DUCKTAIL
FRISETTE
PIGTAILS
PONYTAIL

9-letter words
ARTICHOKE
POMPADOUR

PUZZLE OF THRONES

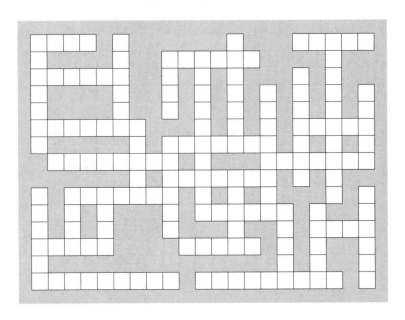

4-letter words
ARYA
OSHA
ROBB
SHAE
YARA

5-letter words
AEMON
DORAN
EURON
GILLY
LUWIN
MEERA
ROOSE
SANSA
VARYS

6-letter words
BENJEN
CERSEI
LYANNA
RAMSAY
RICKON
TALISA
TOMMEN

7-letter words
CATELYN
ELLARIA
PYCELLE
RHAEGAR
SAMWELL
STANNIS
TORMUND
YGRITTE

8-letter words
DAENERYS
PYAT PREE

9-letter words
MISSANDEI
NIGHT KING

10-letter words
MERYN TRANT
WALDER FREY

THE GREAT WHITE NORTH

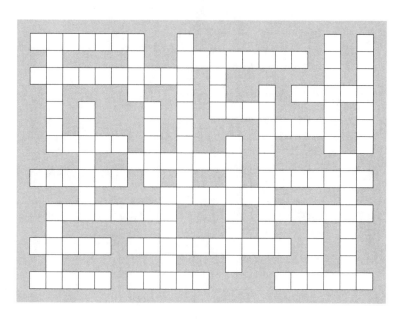

4-letter words
MOIR
RUSH
SCTV

5-letter words
BANFF
DRAKE
GEESE
HOSER
INUIT
LAVAL
MOOSE
SYRUP
TOQUE

6-letter words
OILERS
QUEBEC
REGINA

7-letter words
ALBERTA
CARIBOU
CURLING
HALIFAX
ICE DAMS
ONTARIO
RAPTORS
TIMBITS
TORONTO

8-letter words
DEGRASSI
EDMONTON
LACROSSE
MULRONEY

10-letter words
ALEX TREBEK
BEAVER TAIL
CELINE DION
WHITEHORSE

LA LA LAND

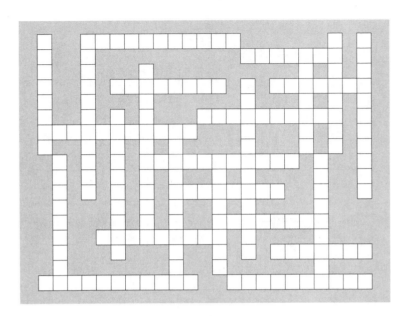

7-letter words
LA JOLLA
LA SCALA
LAST LAP
OOH LA LA

8-letter words
ALAN LADD
BLAH BLAH
FLAGELLA
LAILA ALI
LANDLADY
LAVA LAMP

9-letter words
BALALAIKA
GLADIOLAS
LASH LARUE

10-letter words
FLAVOR FLAV
PLANCK'S LAW
WALLA WALLA

11-letter words
BLACK LAGOON
ILANA GLAZER
LAMAZE CLASS
LAPIS LAZULI
LATEST FLAME
LAWFUL CLAIM
PETULA CLARK

12-letter words
LA ISLA BONITA
POLAR GLACIER

A SKETCHY GROUP

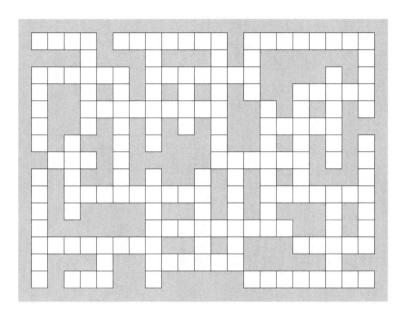

3-letter words
CHE
DAY
FEY

4-letter words
DUNN
MOHR
SANZ

5-letter words
BAYER
CHASE
GUEST
OTERI
SHORT
SLATE

6-letter words
BRYANT
LOVITZ
MEYERS
NEALON
PEDRAD
PRAGER
RADNER

7-letter words
ARMISEN
AYKROYD
BENNETT
HARTMAN
KROEGER
MEADOWS
PISCOPO
SAMBERG
SHEARER

8-letter words
DAVIDSON
GAROFALO
GASTEYER
MOYNIHAN
SUDEIKIS
THOMPSON

9-letter words
CLEGHORNE
O'DONOGHUE
SCHNEIDER

SAY IT!

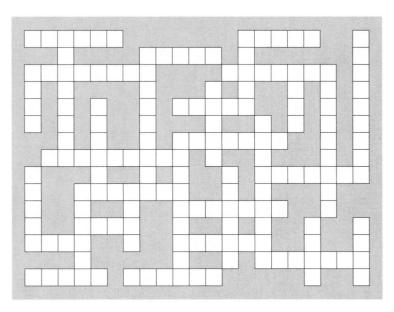

4-letter words
AVOW
CALL
CHAT
CROW
RANT
TALK
TELL

5-letter words
BLURT
BOAST
MIMIC
OPINE
ORATE
QUOTE
VOICE

6-letter words
ASSERT
CLAMOR
HOLLER
PATTER
PIPE UP
YAMMER

7-letter words
DICTATE
EXCLAIM
EXPLAIN
NARRATE
PROTEST
RESPOND

8-letter words
ANNOUNCE
CONVERSE

9-letter words
DISCOURSE
ELUCIDATE
ENUNCIATE
REITERATE
SERMONIZE
VERBALIZE

FILM FESTIVAL

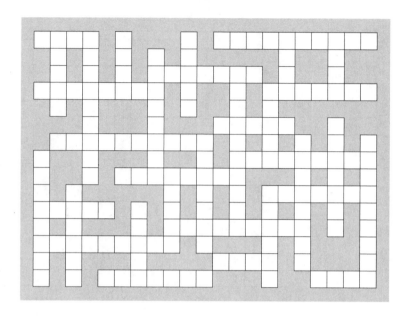

4-letter words
FAME
GIGI
JAWS
JUNO
MASH
TRON

5-letter words
ALFIE
CRASH
FARGO
GHOST
GIGLI
MARTY
SELMA

6-letter words
HARVEY
PSYCHO

7-letter words
AIRPORT
NETWORK
PLATOON
SERPICO
STRIPES
TITANIC

8-letter words
ADAM'S RIB
CHOCOLAT
CIMARRON
KING KONG
MAGNOLIA

9-letter words
BRING IT ON
GLADIATOR
LOVE STORY
STAGE DOOR
THE PLAYER

10-letter words
GOLDFINGER
GOODFELLAS
RAGING BULL

MAMMAL MANIA

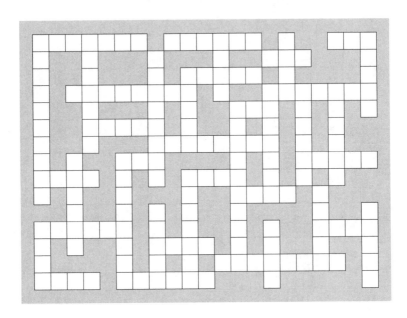

3-letter words
APE
BAT
GNU
PIG

4-letter words
GOAT
IBEX
KUDU
LION
LYNX
MINK
MOLE
PACA
PIKA
SEAL

5-letter words
CAMEL
ELAND
LEMUR
SABLE
SHEEP
SKUNK
TAKIN
TIGER

6-letter words
COYOTE
FERRET
QUOKKA
SEA COW
WAPITI
WOMBAT

7-letter words
CHAMOIS
GAZELLE
MACAQUE
MANATEE
MUNTJAC

8-letter words
AARDWOLF
ELEPHANT
JAVELINA
MANDRILL
REINDEER

10-letter words
CHINCHILLA
GIANT PANDA

BECAUSE THEY'RE THERE

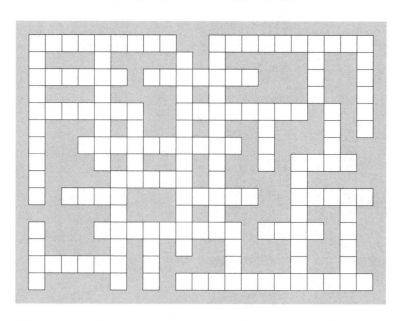

4-letter words
ALPS
EMEI
ETNA
FUJI
HOOD
K-TWO
NEBO
OSSA
TODI

5-letter words
KENYA
LOGAN
SINAI
TABLE

6-letter words
ARARAT
ELBRUS
LHOTSE
TETONS

7-letter words
EVEREST
KAILASH
WHITNEY

8-letter words
BEN NEVIS
HALF DOME
ST. HELENS

9-letter words
EL CAPITAN
MONT BLANC

10-letter words
KIRKJUFELL
MATTERHORN
PIZ BERNINA

12-letter words
KANCHENJUNGA
POPOCATEPETL
VINSON MASSIF

IN THE ROCK & ROLL HALL OF FAME

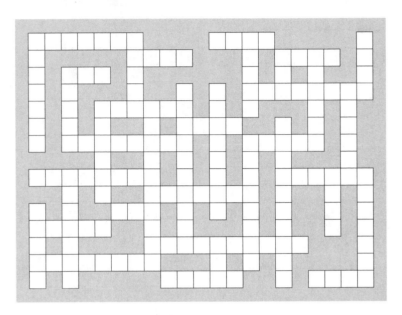

3-letter words
CCR
CSN
NWA
REM

4-letter words
ABBA
(The) CARS
(Duane) EDDY
KISS
(Darlene) LOVE
RHCP
RUSH

5-letter words
(Solomon) BURKE
(Jimmy) CLIFF

CREAM
(The) DOORS
ELVIS (Presley)
HEART
(Bonnie) RAITT

6-letter words
(Tupac) SHAKUR
(Percy) SLEDGE
(Donna) SUMMER
(James) TAYLOR
THE WHO

7-letter words
(Neil) DIAMOND
NIRVANA
(The) RASCALS
THE BAND
TRAFFIC

8-letter words
BOB DYLAN
(Aretha)
    FRANKLIN
(Smokey)
    ROBINSON
(The) RONETTES
TOM PETTY
(The) VENTURES

10-letter words
FRANK ZAPPA
ISAAC HAYES
MILES DAVIS
(The)
    PRETENDERS

ROOM FOR EVERYONE

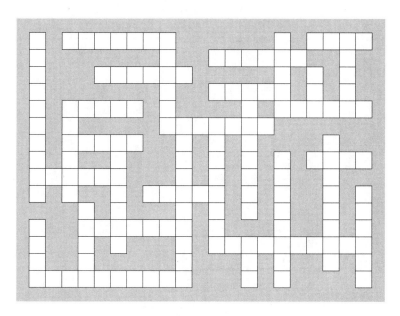

3-letter words
DEN
GYM

4-letter words
CELL
HALL
LOFT

5-letter words
ATTIC
FOYER
LANAI
SALON
SAUNA
SUITE
VAULT

6-letter words
ARMORY
ATRIUM
GARRET
PANTRY
SHRINE
SKYWAY
VESTRY

7-letter words
ATELIER
MAN CAVE
THEATER
VERANDA

8-letter words
CATACOMB
LAVATORY
WARDROBE
WORKSHOP

10-letter words
AUDITORIUM
BEDCHAMBER
GREENHOUSE
LIVING ROOM

SWARM OF B'S

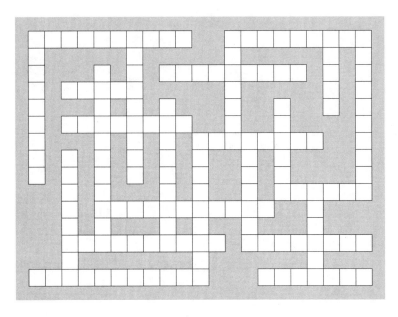

5-letter words
BOBBY
BUBBA

6-letter words
BAOBAB
BOBBIN
HUBBUB

7-letter words
BABBITT
BLUBBER
BUG BOMB

8-letter words
BABY BOOM
BARABBAS
BIT BY BIT
PLUMB BOB

9-letter words
BEELZEBUB
BIBLE BELT
BILL BIXBY
BUD ABBOTT
BUMBLEBEE
ROBIN GIBB

10-letter words
BLUE RIBBON
BUBBLE BATH
BURN RUBBER

11-letter words
ABDUL-JABBAR
BARBI BENTON
BASEBALL BAT

MATERIAL EVIDENCE

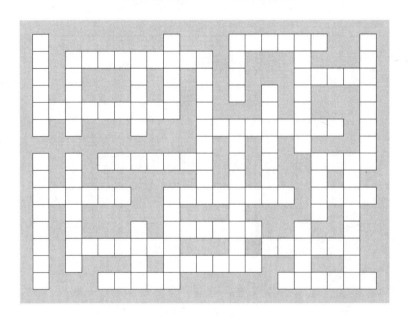

4-letter words
FELT
FLAX
JUTE
LACE
LAMÉ
MESH

5-letter words
BATIK
MOIRÉ
PIQUE
RAMIE
SCRIM

6-letter words
ALPACA
BOUCLÉ
COTTON
DAMASK
FLEECE
KERSEY
MOHAIR
SATEEN

7-letter words
BATISTE
CAMBRIC
ORGANZA
PERCALE
TAFFETA

8-letter words
CASHMERE
CHENILLE
DUNGAREE
JACQUARD

9-letter words
BOMBAZINE
CRINOLINE
GABARDINE
GROSGRAIN
SHEARLING

ROMANS AND GREEKS

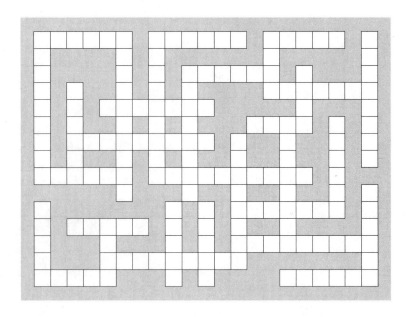

4-letter words
CATO
HERO
LIVY
OTHO

5-letter words
AESOP
HOMER
LIVIA
LUCAN
PLINY
SOLON

6-letter words
BRUTUS
CAESAR
CICERO
EUCLID
PINDAR
SAPPHO
SENECA
TRAJAN

7-letter words
OCTAVIA
PLAUTUS
TACITUS

8-letter words
DOMITIAN
MENANDER
PLUTARCH
TIBERIUS

9-letter words
ARISTOTLE
CALPURNIA
EURIPIDES
JUSTINIAN
VESPASIAN

10-letter words
ARCHIMEDES
DIOCLETIAN

ALL THE MONEY IN THE WORLD

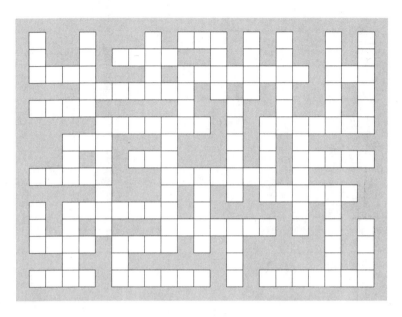

3-letter words
EMU
KIP
LAT
LEK
SEN
SOM
SOU
YEN

4-letter words
BAHT
DIME
EURO
INTI
KINA
MILL
OBOL
PESO

RAND
RIAL
TAKA
YUAN

5-letter words
COLON
DINAR
GROAT
LEONE
TENGE
TOLAR

6-letter words
BALBOA
DALASI
DOLLAR
ESCUDO

GOURDE
NICKEL
PATACA

7-letter words
AFGHANI
AUSTRAL
BITCOIN
CENTAVO
GUARANI
GUILDER
LEMPIRA
METICAL
OUGUIYA

8-letter words
DENARIUS
DOUBLOON

THE I'S HAVE IT

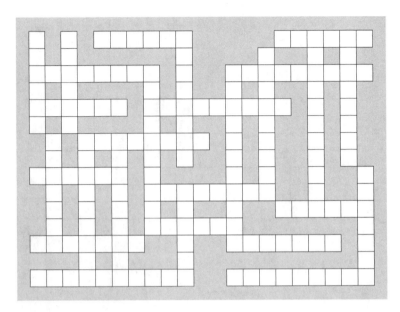

6-letter words
BIKINI
CHI-CHI
FRIGID
ICINGS
KIBITZ
LILITH
MISFIT
TRI-TIP
WIN-WIN

7-letter words
GIMMICK
PILGRIM
PITCH IN
TBILISI

8-letter words
DIMINISH
LINCHPIN
TRIFFIDS
TWILIGHT
WISH LIST

9-letter words
DRINK IT IN
HINDSIGHT
SKINFLINT
THINK THIN
TIGHT-KNIT
WHIRLIGIG

10-letter words
FRIGHT WIGS
NIHILISTIC

11-letter words
BRITISHISMS
DRILLING RIG

BARD EXAM

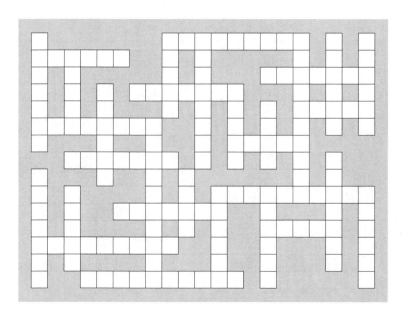

4-letter words
IAGO
KENT

5-letter words
EDGAR
EGEUS
FESTE
PRIAM
SNOUT
SPEED
TIMON

6-letter words
ALONSO
CASSIO
EDMUND
HAMLET
HENRY V
OBERON
TAMORA

7-letter words
CALIBAN
GONZALO
LEONTES
MALCOLM
MIRANDA
PROTEUS
SHYLOCK

8-letter words
BENEDICK
LYSANDER

9-letter words
BRABANTIO
TOBY BELCH

10-letter words
FORTINBRAS
HOLOFERNES
RICHARD III
TOUCHSTONE

PLURALS WITHOUT "S"

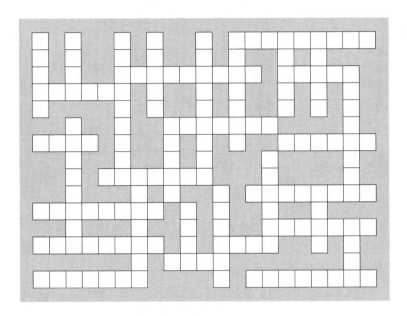

4-letter words
DEER
DICE
FEET
FOCI
FORA
LICE
MICE

5-letter words
CACTI
CELLI
DICTA
GEESE
RADII
SHEEP

6-letter words
GENERA
LARVAE
NUCLEI
STRATA

7-letter words
ADDENDA
CORPORA
SAMURAI
STIMULI
TIMPANI
VISCERA

8-letter words
AIRCRAFT
CHATEAUX
CHILDREN
CRITERIA
GRAFFITI
SERAPHIM

9-letter words
CURRICULA
PAPARAZZI
PHENOMENA
POLYHEDRA

IT'S LIT

4-letter words
BUCK
HUGO

5-letter words
ALGER
CAMUS
CRANE
FRANK
GOGOL
GREER
IBSEN
KEATS
OATES
RILKE
SEUSS
STEIN
WELLS
YEATS

6-letter words
ALCOTT
CARVER
HORNBY
LAHIRI
LEGUIN
MAILER

7-letter words
CHAUCER
LARSSON
LESSING
O'CONNOR
ROBBINS

8-letter words
CHRISTIE
CORNWELL
FAULKNER
STENDHAL

9-letter words
BURROUGHS
PRATCHETT
SOPHOCLES
STEINBECK

OOH!

4-letter words
DREW
GURU
LIEU
MENU
MOUE
OAHU
PERU
POOH
RAGU
ROUX
SHOE

5-letter words
ADIEU
BIJOU
DEBUT
ENSUE
HAIKU
NEHRU
REVUE
SHREW
YAHOO

6-letter words
AVENUE
BAMBOO
CUCKOO
DAEWOO
ESCHEW
FONDUE
PURSUE

7-letter words
MARABOU
OVERDUE
PREVIEW
RESIDUE
SHAMPOO

8-letter words
BALLYHOO
COCKATOO
TIMBUKTU
TIRAMISU

9-letter words
IMPROMPTU
KALAMAZOO

WORLDS APART

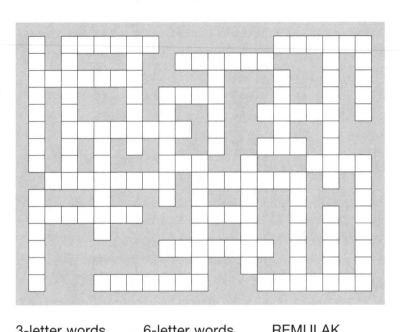

3-letter words
GOR
ORK

4-letter words
HAIN
HOTH
PERN

5-letter words
BAJOR
KOBOL
NABOO
SKARO

6-letter words
CHTHON
MELMAC
SCARIF
TANITH
VULCAN

7-letter words
ACHERON
ANARRES
CAPRICA
DAGOBAH
KRYPTON
MESKLIN
PANDORA

REMULAK
SOLARIS
THERMIA
TRANTOR

8-letter words
ALDERAAN
BARRAYAR
HYPERION
KASHYYYK
TATOOINE

9-letter words
CYBERTRON
MAGRATHEA

WHAT'S THE BIG IKEA?

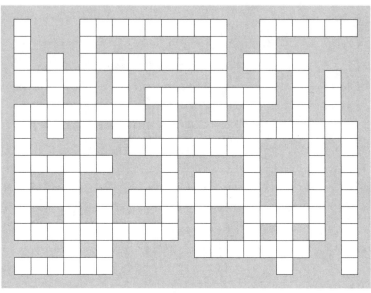

4-letter words
EKET
LACK
LEKA
MÅLA

5-letter words
ALÄNG
DYNAN
HINDÖ
KVART
MULIG
SAMLA
TJENA
VÄDDÖ

6-letter words
GALANT
KUNGSÖ
SENIOR
SOCKER
TOFTAN

7-letter words
KLÄMMIG
ORDNING
SKOGSTA
SPRINGA

8-letter words
FRISKHET
SATSUMAS
SILVERÅN
VADHOLMA
VILDAPEL

9-letter words
ANILINARE
AVSIKTLIG
BESTÅENDE
BJÖRKSNÄS
SÖDERHAMN

10-letter words
MASTHOLMEN
SAMMANHANG

ALTERNATORS

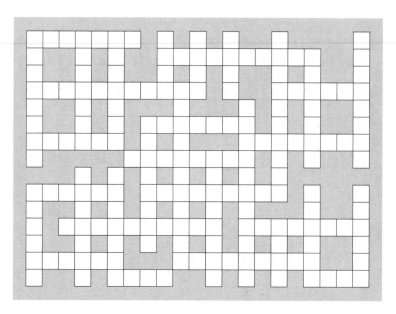

4-letter words
ALAS
COLA
EDIT
EMUS
IBIS
XENA

6-letter words
AVATAR
BANANA
BONITO
CORONA
OBERON
TOMATO
UNIVAC

7-letter words
CAFE CAR
CALIBAN
EPICURE
ERASURE
ON A DARE
PARADOX
REGIMEN

8-letter words
AVOCADOS
EMOTICON
LIBERACE
OCARINAS
ONE-LINER
OVERUSED
TAXI FARE

9-letter words
ESOTERICA
INAMORATA

10-letter words
COPACABANA
MOBILE HOME
VIVA LA VIDA

11-letter words
IMAGINATIVE
SELENA GOMEZ
TELEKINESIS

NOBEL PURSUITS

3-letter words
CHU
PAZ

4-letter words
GORE
HAHN
HULL
KING
ROOT

5-letter words
ANNAN
ARIAS
BEGIN
DYLAN
ELIOT

FERMI
HESSE
LLOSA
MUNRO
OBAMA
PAULI
RABIN
SADAT
YEATS

6-letter words
ARAFAT
HEANEY
O'NEILL
SARTRE
UNICEF
WIESEL

7-letter words
COETZEE
MAHFOUZ
MARCONI
MARQUEZ
WALCOTT

8-letter words
ISHIGURO
RED CROSS
ROENTGEN

9-letter words
BECQUEREL
YOUSAFZAI

COMPUTER GAME

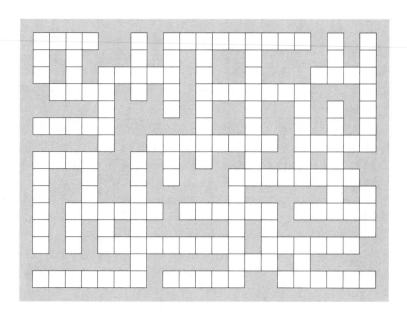

3-letter words
APP
CPU
GIF
IBM
ISP
LAN
MAC
OCR

4-letter words
CHIP
CODE
DATA
DISK
ICON
JAVA
LOOP
PERL

5-letter words
ASCII
BASIC
BATCH
ENIAC
LOGIN
MODEM
VIRUS

6-letter words
CURSOR
GLITCH
INKJET
ONLINE
PROMPT
SCROLL

7-letter words
BOOLEAN
END USER
FORTRAN
PENTIUM
POWER UP

8-letter words
BETA TEST
FUNCTION
GRAPHICS
TOUCH PAD

9-letter words
ALGORITHM
INTERFACE
MAINFRAME

INITIAL HERE AND HERE

6-letter words
C.P. SNOW
H.L. HUNT
J.J. CALE
K.D. LANG

7-letter words
C.S. LEWIS
H.G. WELLS
I.F. STONE
P.D. JAMES
R.L. STINE
W.B. YEATS
W.H. AUDEN

8-letter words
D.B. COOPER
P.J. HARVEY

9-letter words
B.F. SKINNER
H.L. MENCKEN
J.M. COETZEE
S.S. VAN DINE
W.K. KELLOGG
W.S. GILBERT

10-letter words
H.R. HALDEMAN
J.D. SALINGER
J.R.R. TOLKIEN
S.I. HAYAKAWA
S.J. PERELMAN
W.P. KINSELLA

OH, GODS

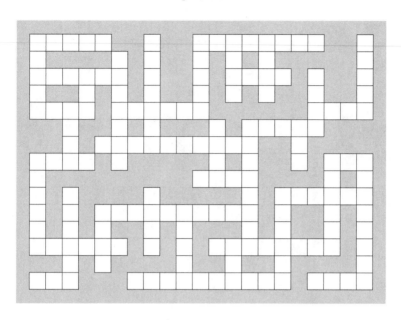

3-letter words	PTAH	SELENE
EOS	RHEA	TETHYS
HEL	TIAN	XOLOTL
NUT		
OPS	5-letter words	7-letter words
SET	DIANA	DEMETER
	HORUS	NEPTUNE
4-letter words	JANUS	
AMUN	THOTH	8-letter words
ARES	VENUS	DIONYSUS
ATEN	VESTA	HYPERION
BAST		POSEIDON
EROS	6-letter words	THANATOS
GAIA	APOLLO	
ISIS	BRAHMA	10-letter words
KALI	HELIOS	HEPHAESTUS
MARS	HESTIA	INARI OKAMI
PELE	SATURN	PROMETHEUS

NAMES FROM FAR, FAR AWAY

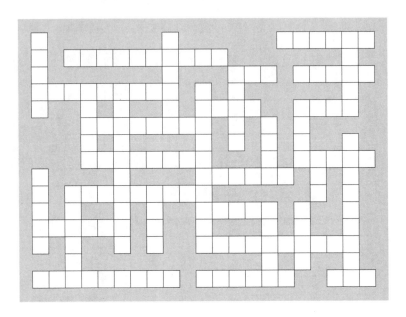

3-letter words
HAN
POE
REY

4-letter words
BERU
FINN
LEIA
LUKE
OOLA
YODA

5-letter words
ARTOO
BIGGS
BOSSK
LANDO
LOBOT
PADME
TEEBO
WATTO
WEDGE

6-letter words
GREEDO
JAR JAR
OBI-WAN
TARKIN
TAUN WE
TEY HOW

8-letter words
GRIEVOUS
SLOWEN LO

9-letter words
DARTH MAUL
JANGO FETT
PONDA BABA
SIO BIBBLE

10-letter words
BAIL ORGANA
BREN DERLIN
SAW GERRERA
SY SNOOTLES

JUST MY CUP OF T

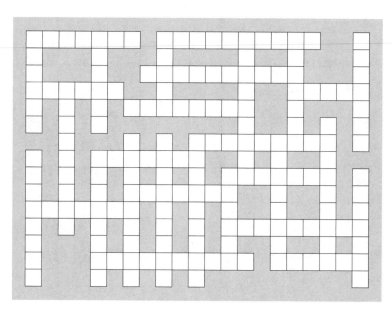

GOTTA CATCH 'EM ALL

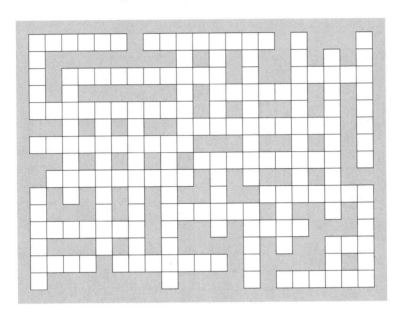

3-letter words
MEW
MUK

4-letter words
ABRA
ONIX
UXIE

5-letter words
BUDEW
HOOPA
RIOLU
TEPIG

6-letter words
BONSLY
DIALGA
LUXRAY
ODDISH
PALKIA
SPEWPA
WEEDLE

7-letter words
AURORUS
HAUNTER
WAILORD
XERNEAS

8-letter words
CHIMCHAR
OSHAWOTT
SQUIRTLE

9-letter words
ALOMOMOLA
MARSHADOW
SANDSHREW
STOUTLAND
TYRANTRUM

10-letter words
CARRACOSTA
CHANDELURE
CONKELDURR
ELECTIVIRE
FERALIGATR
INCINEROAR
WHIMSICOTT

TRIPLE ANAGRAMS

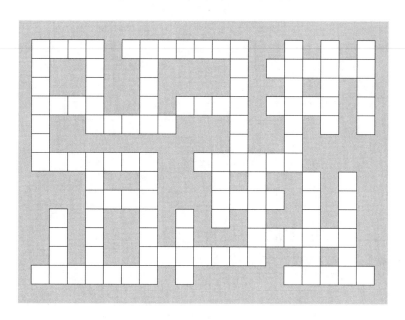

4-letter words	5-letter words	7-letter words
ACRE	ARIES	ANGRIER
CARE	ARISE	EARRING
RACE	RAISE	REARING
EMIT	ESTER	ANTSIER
ITEM	TERSE	RETAINS
TIME	TREES	STAINER
LIEN	6-letter words	ENLARGE
LINE	AVERTS	GENERAL
NILE	STARVE	GLEANER
	VASTER	
	FILTER	
	LIFTER	
	TRIFLE	

NOT ENOUGH VOWELS

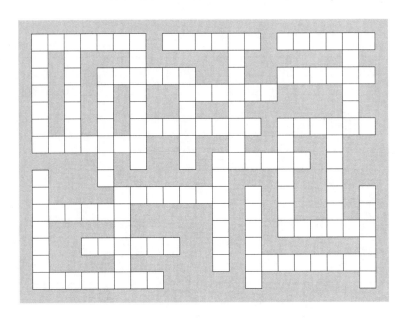

6-letter words
BBQ PIT
BLURBS
DIRNDL
FM BAND
GDANSK
KGB SPY
R. CRUMB
RHYTHM
RUN-DMC
RV PARK
SCHUSS

SCRUFF
STITCH
THIRST
TROGGS

7-letter words
BORSCHT
DR. SPOCK
G-STRING
KLATSCH
MR. RIGHT
NBC NEWS

SCHMIDT
SCHWINN
THWARTS
TSK-TSKS

8-letter words
LGBT FLAG
MGM GRAND
SCHMALTZ
STRENGTH
TWELFTHS

TOO MANY VOWELS

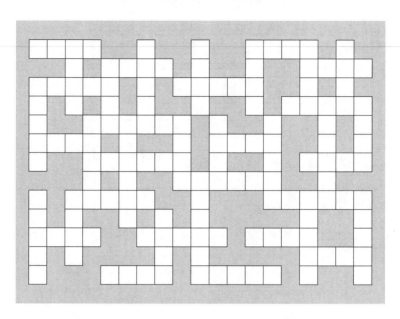

4-letter words
AGUE
AIDE
AIWA
AQUA
AREA
ASIA
AUTO
CIAO
GAIA
IAGO
IDEA
JOEY
KAYO
LEIA
MAUI

OJAI
OKAY
OPIE
OREO
QEII
WII U
YETI

5-letter words
ADIEU
AIOLI
AUDIO
"BOO-YA!"
EAZY-E
EUBIE
GOOEY

KAUAI
OUIJA
"SEE YA"
YAHOO
YAZOO
ZOOEY

6-letter words
AEOLIA
EEYORE
"HEY, YOU!"
INOUYE
OISEAU
YO-YOED
YO-YO MA

X MARKS THE STOP

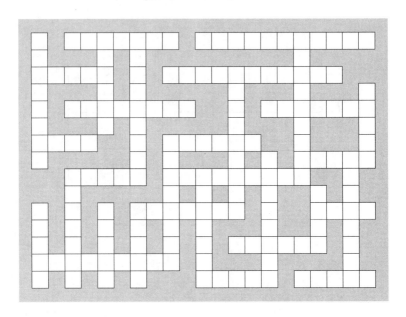

4-letter words
AJAX
JINX
ONYX

5-letter words
CODEX
CTRL-X
EX-LAX
FEDEX
PHLOX
RELAX
ROLEX
VIOXX
XEROX

6-letter words
MATRIX
TEX-MEX
TJ MAXX

7-letter words
ALTO SAX
ASTERIX
CINEMAX
PHOENIX
PLAYTEX

8-letter words
AEON FLUX
FORT KNOX
MAGNAVOX
THE BRONX
TRAIL MIX

9-letter words
EMAIL HOAX
GRAND PRIX
HARPO MARX
HEAT INDEX
RIVER STYX

11-letter words
DOUBLE HELIX
JIMI HENDRIX

ALL THE WAY DOWN

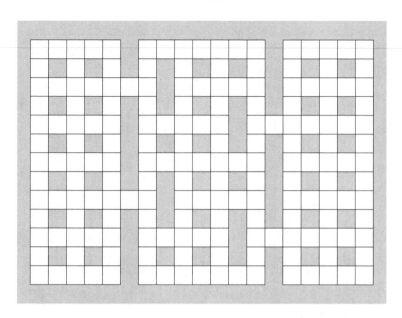

5-letter words	VALOR	13-letter words
AMAZE	VESTS	KARL LAGERFELD
DOGIE	VISIT	KELLY CLARKSON
ICIER		SABER-RATTLING
INAPT	7-letter words	SPRAY-PAINTING
LATTE	BONJOUR	STAY THE COURSE
NOBEL	FADES IN	TALK OF THE
OBESE	MAGICAL	TOWN
RARER	NORWALK	TAPE RECORDERS
REPEL	SHAPIRO	VENETIAN BLIND
SAGAN	YAKUTSK	VENUS WILLIAMS
TRYST	"YES OR NO?"	YAKOV SMIRNOFF

GETTING EVEN

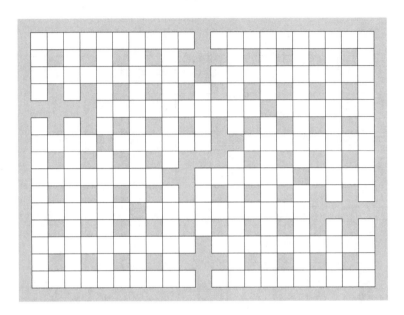

4-letter words
BARD
BARK
FILM
ICON
LPGA
NEMO
SKID
TIVO
UCLA
X-RAY

6-letter words
ARCADE
ARNOLD
ARROYO
ASTUTE
BROKEN
REGGAE
RUN-DMC
SILVER

8-letter words
ACCURATE
MASTODON
OLD SPICE
PAPER CUT
RAGNAROK
SOY SAUCE

10-letter words
BEANIE BABY
FENWAY PARK
HOLY TOLEDO
I WON'T DANCE
JANE AUSTEN
KOOL-AID MAN
LA TRAVIATA
LEMON WEDGE
MITSUBISHI
PUERTO RICO
RUBIK'S CUBE
SKETCH PADS
STORM CLOUD
TAX BRACKET
TED KENNEDY
VINTAGE CAR

THAT'S ODD

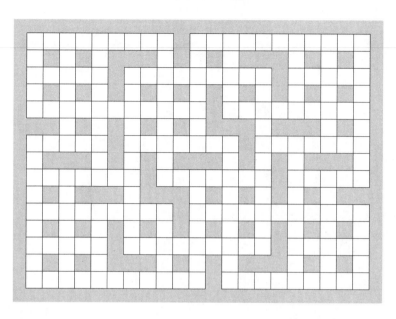

5-letter words
CAJUN
EAGER
EPOCH
EVOKE
JUMBO
NOVAK
REALM
REHAB
RUBLE
SPEAR
VOLVO
WINGS

7-letter words
AIMLESS
HEAR OUT
HOTSHOT
LAMP OIL
MEG RYAN
SCHERZO
STAND-IN
SUBZERO
VIDALIA
VIVALDI

9-letter words
CLIPBOARD
LOWERCASE
MACINTOSH
OZONE HOLE

SEMISWEET
SORE LOSER
TIDAL POOL
TOOTHPICK
TWIN PEAKS
VANCOUVER
WATERGATE
WESTWORLD

11-letter words
COUCH POTATO
DICK VAN DYKE
DO THE DISHES
MOLLYCODDLE
ROYAL PURPLE
SIR LANCELOT

5, 6, 7, 8

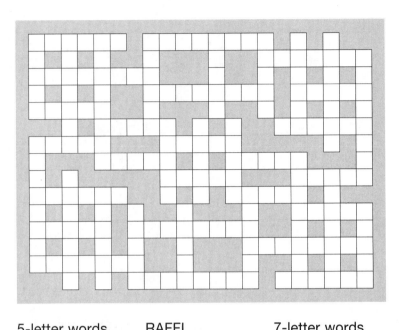

5-letter words
BAYOU
BLAST
BRAVO
CHICO
GIZMO
HONOR
JOSIE
KAFKA
KUGEL
MANOR
NOKIA
'N SYNC
ONE P.M.
ORGAN
PESKY

RAFFI
R AND B
SNAKE
TEETH
THINK
ZAGAT

6-letter words
CHANEL
EXURBS
FRESCA
IMPROV
ROTHKO
SELFIE
SLAYER
SPYCAM

7-letter words
ELPHABA
FRENEMY
LAZY EYE
ROY G. BIV
SALIERI
TIP JARS

8-letter words
ALOE VERA
FOURTEEN
FRUIT CUP
JUICE BAR
KIBITZER
NYPD BLUE
OK CORRAL
OVALTINE
RAPUNZEL
STAR TREK

AT THE 7-11

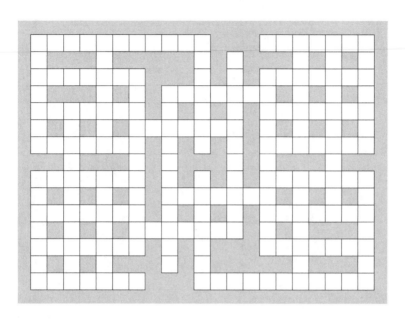

7-letter words
ASPIRIN
BATCAVE
BERTRAM
BUFFALO
DOZE OFF
EARPLUG
ENZYMES
EXTINCT
GARLAND
HARRIET
MAZURKA
NITPICK

OPOSSUM
ORGANIC
PAPAYAS
PLATEAU
PRAIRIE
RIDDLES
RITALIN
SALIERI
SHAMPOO
SOLOIST
SPRAY-ON
ST. REGIS
TROTSKY

TURN RED
TWO-STEP
YULE LOG

11-letter words
BOB'S BURGERS
CAPTAIN KIRK
DINOSAUR EGG
JUST MARRIED
LORETTA LYNN
MYTHBUSTERS
PIZZA PARLOR
TROJAN HORSE

FIVE AND DIME

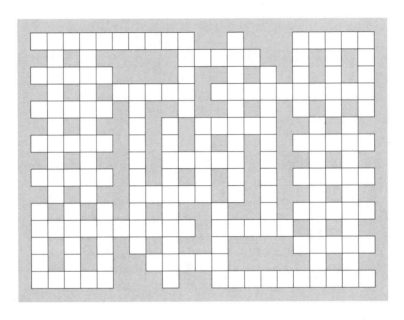

5-letter words
BRISK
CAMEL
COSMO
CROWD
DECAF
FRITO
FROCK
HONDA
HONOR
HYPER
IBSEN
LASER
MAGIC

MAVEN
MIX-UP
MOCHA
NOISY
POLYP
PSYCH
RELAX
RHINO
SCHWA
SCONE
STEAM
VOGUE
WALL-E

10-letter words
AFTER HOURS
BARNEY FIFE
BENDY STRAW
BUCKET SEAT
CALL IT A DAY
CURLY FRIES
GOLF COURSE
HELLO KITTY
JELLY DONUT
SCUBA DIVER
TAMAGOTCHI
THE WOLFMAN

10-4, GOOD BUDDY

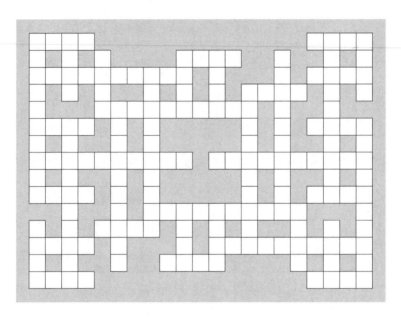

4-letter words	NINE	10-letter words
ABC'S	ODIN	ARMORED CAR
AHAB	OOPS	DUMBLEDORE
AMEN	PAST	ELMER'S GLUE
ANKH	RENO	FROZEN FOOD
BULB	SKIM	I OWE YOU ONE
EURO	SPUR	IPHONE APPS
EXAM	SUEZ	LEDERHOSEN
EXEC	SULU	L. FRANK BAUM
KISS	WOLF	MITSUBISHI
MEEK	WREN	P.S. I LOVE YOU
MEWL	YEAR	PURPLE HAZE
NAIF		ROLEX WATCH
		SIS BOOM BAH
		TESLA COILS

7-10 SPLIT

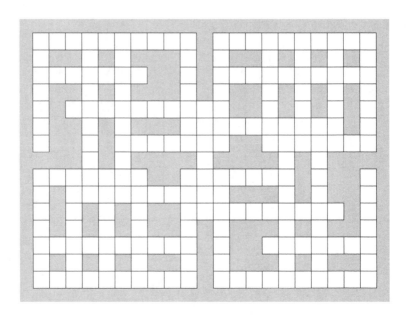

7-letter words
AIRFARE
ALFALFA
BERSERK
COPILOT
CURTAIL
"EN GARDE!"
EQUATOR
EXPRESS
EYE TEST
FINESSE

GARBAGE
"GLORY BE!"
ISOLATE
MISS USA
NO CARBS
O CANADA
PERRIER
RED BULL
SANTA FE
SHINGLE
SOMEHOW

10-letter words
BIG BAD WOLF
EAST OF EDEN
FREE REFILL
GENOME MAPS
HEAVY METAL
L. FRANK BAUM
LOW-FAT MILK
PADEREWSKI
RAGAMUFFIN
SILLY GOOSE
TERRA FIRMA
TORTELLINI
WHERE IT'S AT
WILLY WONKA

WORKING 9 TO 5

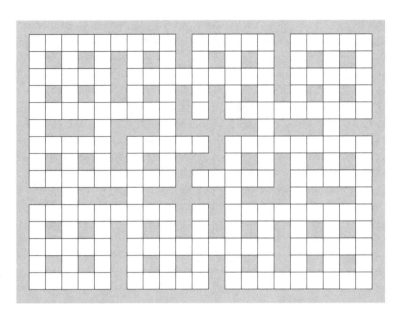

5-letter words
ABDUL
ADELE
BAMBI
BRICK
BUGLE
DISCO
DROID
DUSTY
ELEGY
FUNGI
IDAHO
LIVER
MAD TV
MOOSE
MOTET

MYLAR
NIVEA
OSAKA
Q*BERT
SAUNA
TROUT
UMASS
UNARM
YIKES

9-letter words
A BUG'S LIFE
AISLE SEAT
BEN VEREEN
BLUE APRON
BON VIVANT

COACHELLA
DAFFY DUCK
DOOHICKEY
"DO YOU
    MIND?"
EMAIL HOAX
EMMA STONE
GANGPLANK
GOLD COAST
GOOD KARMA
KOFI ANNAN
NOTRE DAME
NUMBER ONE
PARCHEESI
TRADITION
VOX POPULI

GOOD LUCK AND BAD LUCK

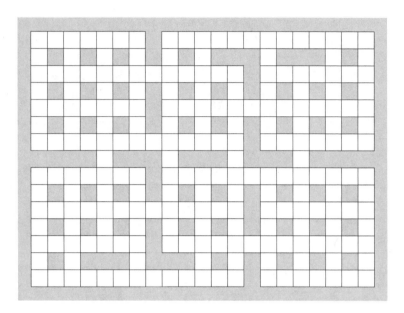

7-letter words	PACE LAP	13-letter words
ANGELOU	POINT AT	EILEEN BRENNAN
ANTENNA	POWDERY	ELVIS COSTELLO
CAB FARE	PYTHONS	FAHRVERGNÜGEN
CHOBANI	REHEATS	IT'S NOT UNUSUAL
DIAMOND	RUN INTO	KENNEBUNKPORT
FLATBED	SCANNED	KICKS UPSTAIRS
IDIOTIC	SWING BY	KNAVE OF HEARTS
IMAGINE	"THAT'S ME!"	"NEEDLESS TO SAY…"
MARCEAU	THREE A.M.	SECRET SOCIETY
OUTDOOR	TOFUTTI	THE LAST TO KNOW
	TOYS "R" US	TRANSPLANTING
		TRIAL BY COMBAT

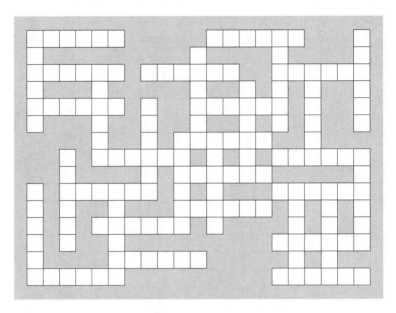

6-letter words

AL CAPP
AL GORE
AT HAND
AT LAST
AU PAIR
BO PEEP
BY JOVE
DE NIRO
DE TROP
DU JOUR
EL NIÑO

EM DASH
ET ALIA
GI BILL
GM FOOD
GO TEAM
IN NEED
IN STIR
IN TOTO
IO MOTH
IT GIRL
LE MANS
MI AMOR

MY WORD
OF LATE
ON TOUR
OR ELSE
PA JOAD
PT BOAT
RC COLA
SO WHAT
ST. IVES
TY COBB
VW BUGS
WU-TANG

SIX-PACK

THE MAGNIFICENT SEVEN

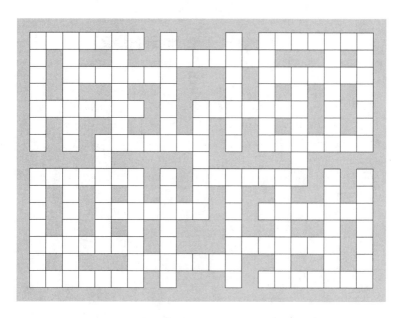

7-letter words
ACOLYTE
AXL ROSE
BATCAVE
BOLO TIE
DONOVAN
"DREAM ON!"
DRUM KIT
ENZYMES
FREEBIE
GAS LEAK
HELIPAD
HIJINKS

ICED TEA
"I GIVE UP"
IN BRIEF
IN STYLE
IQ TESTS
JETBLUE
LIP-SYNC
LUCY LIU
NOXZEMA
OBELISK
PICASSO
POLYMER
RAVIOLI

RAY-O-VAC
SAFFRON
SAVANNA
SHOW BIZ
SLURPEE
SQUEEZE
STAN LEE
SUBZERO
SYNERGY
TRAFFIC
TV GUIDE
YOUTUBE

CRAZY EIGHTS

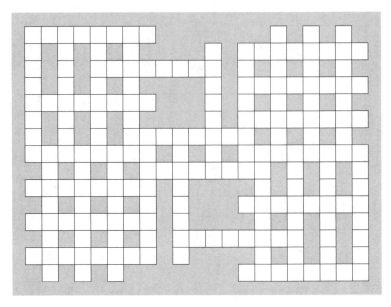

8-letter words

ADAM'S RIB
ALAN ALDA
ALPHA RAY
BEAR CLAW
CARDINAL
CB RADIOS
DON PARDO
DR. WATSON
FACEPALM
FENG SHUI
GO STEADY

GYM SHOES
HAD A BALL
HE'S SO SHY
"I BEFORE E ..."
IOLANTHE
KING KONG
LAVA FLOW
LBJ RANCH
LEAP YEAR
OFFSHOOT
OLYMPICS
OPERA HAT

OUT OF GAS
PETER PAN
REST AREA
ROLL BACK
SEAN PENN
SKI AREAS
TAJ MAHAL
THAILAND
THERAFLU
WAR ZONES
WATER SKI

CRAZIER EIGHTS

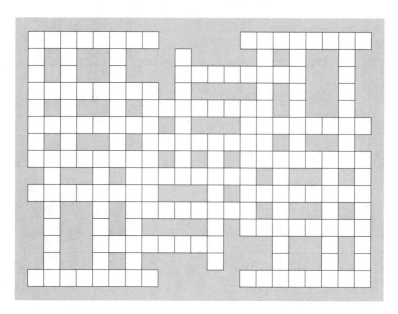

<u>8-letter words</u>
ALPHABET
AMETHYST
APERITIF
BIT BY BIT
COLDPLAY
"DEAL ME IN!"
DISBANDS
ENTITLED
FUEL CELL
HODA KOTB
"I PROMISE"

KEEP COOL
KRAKATOA
LINDY HOP
LIP GLOSS
LYRICIST
MEL BLANC
MR. MIYAGI
NAZARETH
NEPOTISM
OIL BARON
ONE NIGHT
O SOLE MIO

OTTER POP
OUT OF GAS
PEDIGREE
POWER SAW
SHAMEFUL
SLOW LEAK
SUDDENLY
TEST TUBE
UNGAINLY
YMA SUMAC
YOGI BEAR

THE WHOLE NINE YARDS

9-letter words

ANGKOR WAT
ASK AROUND
ASTROLABE
BUBBA GUMP
CLOSE CALL
COWABUNGA
CRO-MAGNON
DEBIT CARD
EQUIPMENT
FACE VALUE
FENCED OFF
FIBONACCI

GIFT OF GAB
"I DON'T CARE"
IN THE LOOP
JAMES BOND
LOUD SHIRT
PENNY LANE
PIXIE CUTS
RIO GRANDE
TAX REFUND
TOWELETTE
TRAY TABLE
VOICE MAIL
"YOU GO, GIRL!"

PERFECT 10

10-letter words
COIN RETURN
DURAN DURAN
E.E. CUMMINGS
FRIGIDAIRE
GOOSEBUMPS
GRASS SKIRT
IN ABSENTIA
JASMINE TEA
J.R.R. TOLKIEN
KOALA BEARS
LAUNDROMAT
MAID MARIAN

MOOD INDIGO
OZZIE SMITH
PUFF PIECES
RARING TO GO
ROOKIE YEAR
TOFU HOT DOG
UNICYCLIST
VANNA WHITE
WATCHWORDS
WEBSURFING
WORK PERMIT
"YES INDEEDY!"

THIS ONE GOES TO 11

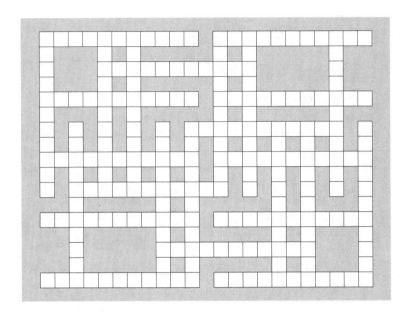

11-letter words

ALL-STAR GAME
AMATEUR HOUR
DAMON RUNYON
EASTER BUNNY
FINDING NEMO
FINGER LAKES
FOOTBALL FAN
GREEN HORNET
GROUCHO MARX
HALLUCINATE
HERE'S JOHNNY
HIGH ANXIETY
HOUSE LIGHTS

HULLABALLOO
JERRY ORBACH
JOIE DE VIVRE
JUMBO SHRIMP
MISANTHROPE
MOSQUITO NET
NOISEMAKERS
ORSON WELLES
OVERPAYMENT
ST. LOUIS ARCH
SYLVIA PLATH
UPHILL CLIMB
VANILLA COKE

ANSWERS

7 MONOPOLIZING THE CONVERSATION

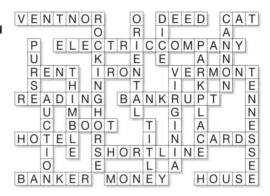

```
V E N T N O R     O   D E E D   C A T
        O         R   I         A
    P   E L E C T R I C C O M P A N Y
    U     K       E     E   A N Y
    R E N T   I R O N     V E R M O N T
    S     H   N   T       I   K N   E
R E A D I N G   B A N K R U P T     N
    U   M   H   L       G   L       N
    C   B O O T     T   I   A       E
H O T E L   R       I   N   C A R D S
    I   E   S H O R T L I N E       S
    O       E       L   A           E
B A N K E R   M O N E Y     H O U S E
```

8 BOWL GAME

```
C H E E R I O S   M I N I W H E A T S
        M       U   O           L
      G R A P E N U T S         P
C H E X     R   S   R       G   E   T
O         T   L   I       O   N   R
R I C E K R I S P I E S       L       I
N   O       T   X   H O N E Y K I X
F   R   T O T A L   S   R   A   A
L   N       R     M   E   N   B   K
A L P H A B I T S   O   O       O   A
K   O           F R O O T L O O P S
E   P U F F I N S   Z   S       M   H
S   S                               I
```

9 MAKEUP TEST

```
K A T V O N D   T W E E Z E R S     M
    O           A     Y             I
A   M O I S T U R I Z E R     D     R
V   F       H   T     B   P R I M E R
O   O   M A T T E     R       O     O
N A R S     D     B R O N Z E R     R
    D   P O M A D E   W       Y
    U       W     N   P A L E T T E
    L U S H   S P O N G E     L     L
    T           Y     E       I     F
M A Y B E L L I N E   C H A N E L
A                     I       E
C O N C E A L E R     L     R O U G E
```

10 COLOR GUARD

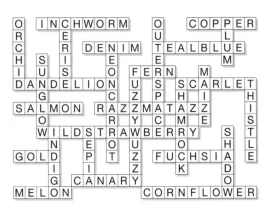

11 DOUBLE DOUBLE-U

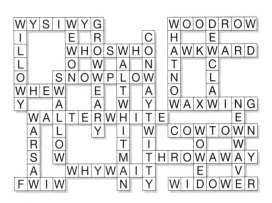

12 MUSICAL ARRANGEMENT

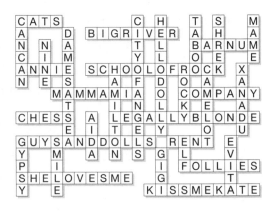

13 JAPANESE IMPORTS

14 MALL DIRECTORY

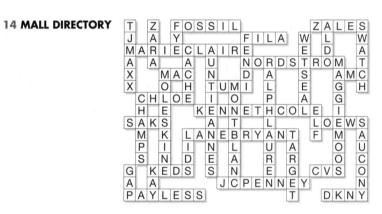

15 R2-D2

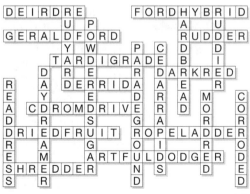

16 LUCY IN THE SKY

17 OZONE

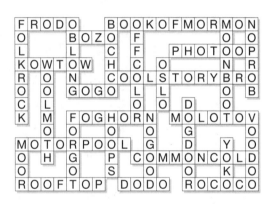

18 SING A SONG OF SONDHEIM

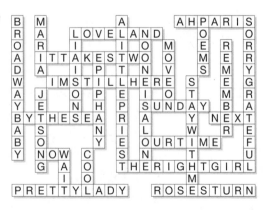

19 HALLOWEEN SCENE

20 WHAT'S THE DEAL?

21 THEY'VE GOT THEIR UPS & DOWNS

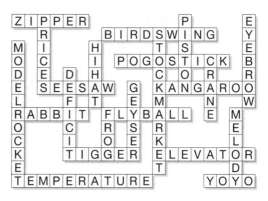

125

22 A PUZZLING PUZZLE

23 SHIPSHAPE

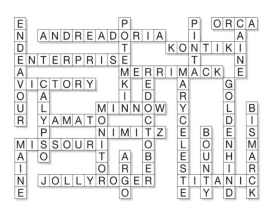

24 GIVE ME A SIGN

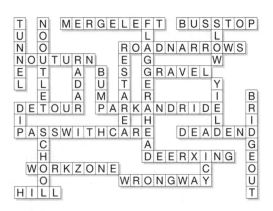

25 EARN YOUR STRIPES

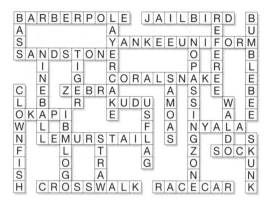

26 TRAFFIC JAM

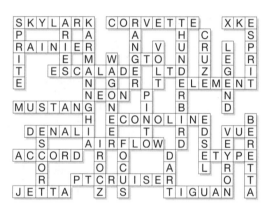

27 EAT UP!

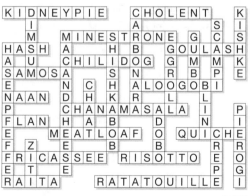

28 BACK AND FORTH

29 IN THE SWIM

30 IT'S TIME TO MEET THE MUPPETS

31 EXCLAMATION STATION

32 DIZZY WITH DISNEY

33 DIZZIER WITH DISNEY

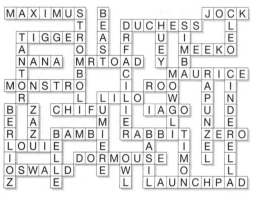

34 WE'RE FROM FRANCE

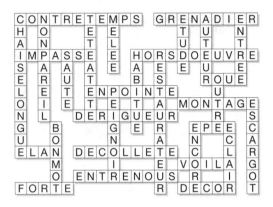

35 SAY "CHEESE"

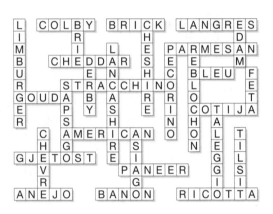

36 ARCADIA

37 COMPOSE YOURSELF

38 HOT STUFF

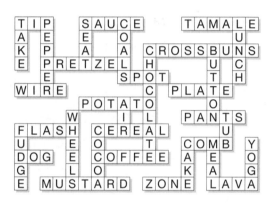

39 MAGAZINE RACK

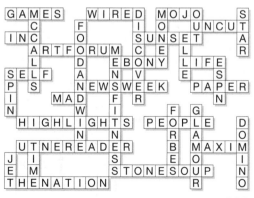

40 HOLIDAYS FROM ALL OVER

41 LOOK! UP IN THE SKY!

42 EPIC FAIL

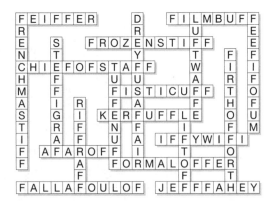

43 FLATLAND

```
C D C A S E   B I R C H B A R K   C A P E
  A           O                   R E   O P
  R       M A G A Z I N E         P     T
P A P E R W   S           A       P     T
H   E     I B T       M O U S E P A D
O T   P A N C A K E   T   H           R
T     D   N   R       O W E L         T
O   P L Y W O O D     A       E
S A   W A             G     T I L E
T M R P I     P T             E   F
R P L A C A R D   T S Q U A R E   F
I H F N       A B   C       F     L
P A L E T T E   B I L L B O A R D   T
  E         N   E       R
F U T O N   R E C E I P T   F O L D E R
```

44 PITCH PERFECT

```
D   Z   R       Y               W Y N N
R   I   Y   V I O L A     C O N E     M
A   T   A       U   L             B   M
B R O W N   L I N C E C U M       B L U E
E           G   X       A             S
K E R S H A W     C A R L T O N       S
I           A     N       H   I       I
G A G N E   D R Y S D A L E   E       N
H           D     E     W   K A A T
B U E H R L E   F O R D   S   R       I
    T   L         E   O D O M         A
    T   L       S P A H N             N
G U I D R Y             N     H O Y T
```

45 RHYME TIME

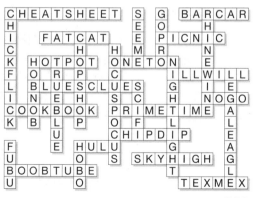

```
C H E A T S H E E T   S   G     B A R C A R
H                     E   O         H
I     F A T C A T     E   P I C N I C   N
C             H   H   M   R         N
K   H O T P O T   O N E T O N       E
F   O   R   P     C           I L L W I L L
L   B L U E S C L U E S   G     I     E
I   N   E   H     S   C   H     N O G O
C O O K B O O K   P R I M E T I M E   A
K   B   L   P     O   F   L           L
    U         C H I P D I P           E
F   E   H U L U   U   G               A
U       O   S     S K Y H I G H       G
B O O B T U B E       T               L
U       O           T E X M E X
```

133

46 SCHOOL SPIRIT

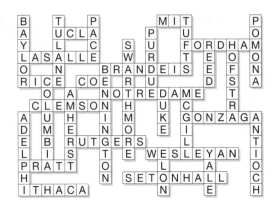

47 MEASURING UP

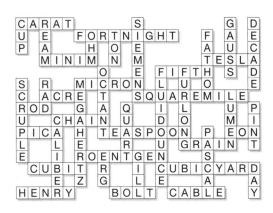

48 TOO WISE

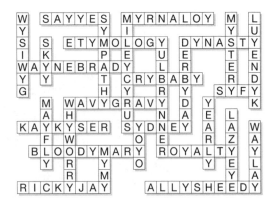

134

49 TEAMWORK

```
C A R D I N A L S   W I N G S   S T O R M
A   A       E       T       A   K       E
V   N       T   R E D B U L L S Y       T
A N G E L S     E   U   A   R   R A M S
L   E   I       L   C   X   A       A
I   R   G   M E R C U R Y   P       V
E   S   H       R   A   A   I       E
R       T W I N S   N   P R E D A T O R S
S   S U N   M   H E A T     S       I
    I       P       E   O   D   J   C
H   B E N G A L S   R   R   Y   E   K
A   I   G   C   P   S   S E N A T O R S
W I L D     T   U       A       S
K   L       R           M
S   S   C O L T S       R E V O L U T I O N
```

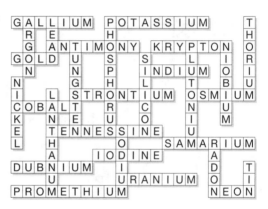

```
G A L L I U M   P O T A S S I U M       T
  R   E         H                       H
  G   A N T I M O N Y   K R Y P T O N   O
G O L D   U     S   S       L   I       R
  N   N   N     P   I N D I U M   O     I
N     G   G     H   L       T   B       U
I   L   S T R O N T I U M   O S M I U M
C O B A L T     R   C       N       U
K   N   E       U   O       I       M
E   T E N N E S S I N E      U
L   H           O       S A M A R I U M
    A       I O D I N E         A
D U B N I U M   I               D       T
    U           U R A N I U M   O       I
P R O M E T H I U M             N E O N
```

```
T R A C Y   S E A V E R         B R A D Y
H           A           B       N
U   P O S T O N   N I L S S O N D
M   O   T         P       S     R E I D
B U T T O N   C L A N C Y L   B R   E
  T   P       T   A       E B E R S O L
  E   P   D A S T A R D L Y R   O   A
M O R G A N   E   A       G N   Y
    R     V A N D Y K E   E
  H O U D I N I   A       P A R T C H
  A       L   S   G       O         C
S M O T H E R S   C O U R T E N A Y L
  L       A   H   E       O         A
  I       C   L I M E   L E H R E R R
E N B E R G   K I T E   N       K   K
```

135

52 THAT'S SUPER

53 RAINING CATS AND DOGS

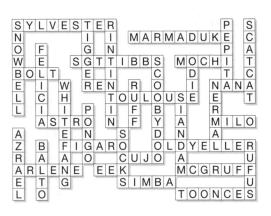

54 CAPITALIZED

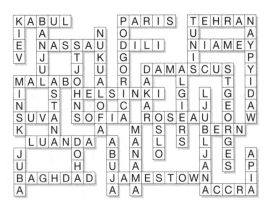

55 RR CROSSING

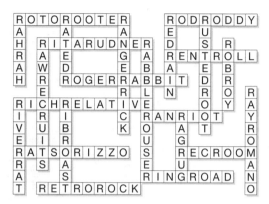

```
R O T O R O O T E R       R O D R O D D Y
R     A     A       E     U
H   R I T A R U D N E R   D   S   R
R   A   E     G   A   R E N T R O L L
A   W   D     E   B   A     E   B
H   R   R O G E R R A B B I T   D   R
    E   R     L   N       R   O   R
R I C H R E L A T I V E   R   O   A
I   R   I       C   R A N R I O T   Y
V   U   B     K   O   A   T       R
E   I   R         U   G   T       O
R A T S O R I Z Z O   S   R E C R O O M
R   S   A         E   U           A
A   S       R I N G R O A D       N
T   R E T R O R O C K             O
```

56 FOR VEGETARIANS

```
C U C U M B E R   A R U G U L A     C O R N
H   H       E           R           H
A   A       L E M O N G R A S S     I   D
Y   R       L       U       P W     C   I
O   D       P   S E S A M E   E     K A L E
T     J     E   H       L E E K     P   L
E     I     P U R S L A N E   T     E
      C     P   O       A S P A R A G U S
J A L A P E N O     A   V   O   O   A
      M     R   M   N   E   T   M O R E L
O K R A       P C A S S A V A   B     E
N     B       E H       T   I   A     N
I     E   Y   A V O C A D O   N   A     T
O L I V E     A             E   Z     I
N     T O M A T I L L O             O   L
```

57 LAUGHING MATTERS

```
J E F F E R S O N S   M I S T E R E D     G
U   E   L             O                   E
S   L   O   W H O S T H E B O S S         T
T   F   O         O     S   F   C   C     S
S   A L F         A     H   F T R O O P   M
H   M   A   R   P   T A X I   U   A       A
O   I   C   O     E     C   B E C K E R   T
O   L   T   S   M U N S T E R S   H
T   Y   S   E   A       A
M Y T W O D A D S   C O U G A R T O W N
E   I   F   N   H   I       I           N
    E L L E N     O   D       V   N     A
M   S   I   E N T O U R A G E   E   G   N
O   O   F         S     E   B E N S O N   Y
M A U D E   B R O A D C I T Y     P       Y
```

58 LET'S DANCE

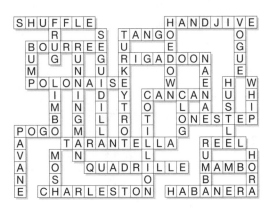

59 TRIAL RUN

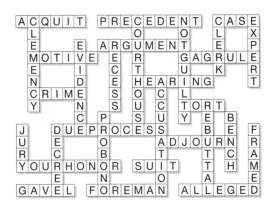

60 INTERIOR DECORATING

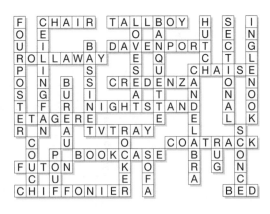

61 MATH APPEAL

62 FLOWER POWER

63 A TRIP TO THE HARDWARE STORE

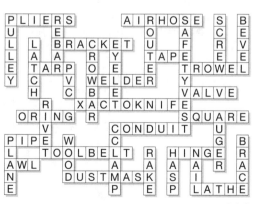

67 HAIR THERE AND EVERYWHERE

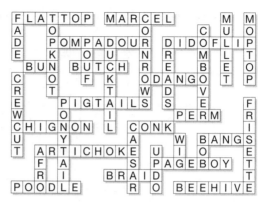

68 PUZZLE OF THRONES

69 THE GREAT WHITE NORTH

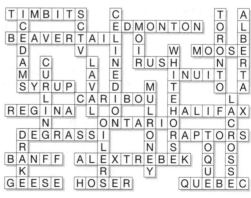

70 LA LA LAND

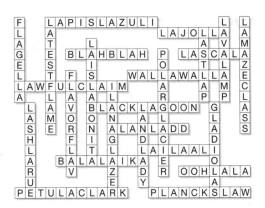

71 A SKETCHY GROUP

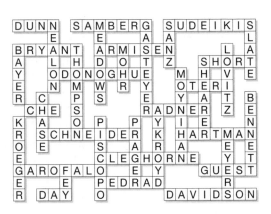

72 SAY IT!

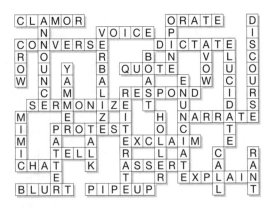

73 FILM FESTIVAL

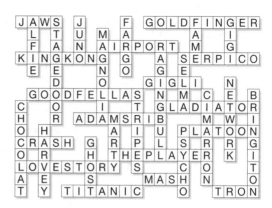

74 MAMMAL MANIA

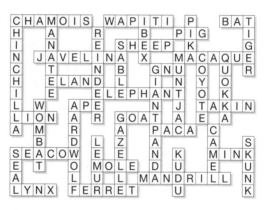

75 BECAUSE THEY'RE THERE

143

76 IN THE ROCK & ROLL HALL OF FAME

77 ROOM FOR EVERYONE

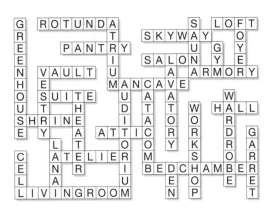

78 SWARM OF B'S

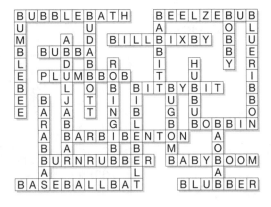

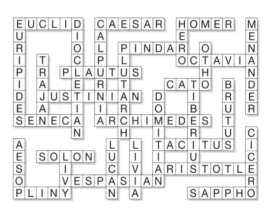

145

82 THE I'S HAVE IT

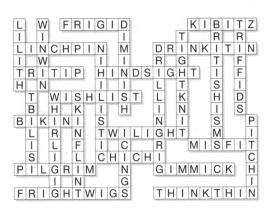

83 BARD EXAM

84 PLURALS WITHOUT "S"

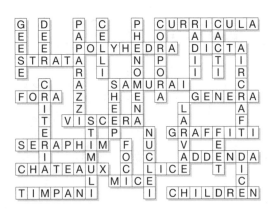

85 IT'S LIT

86 OOH!

87 WORLDS APART

89 ALTERNATORS

90 NOBEL PURSUITS

91 COMPUTER GAME

```
C O D E       D     A L G O R I T H M     M     P
P     A       I     S     R       N             A     E
U T     B A S I C       A       T           I C O N
    J A V A       K       I     P O W E R U P         T
        T             I       H       R       R     E     I
E N I A C             I       F       O       N       U
        H     T O U C H P A D       M O D E M
C H I P     F     C     S       C       P     U
U       E     U     R         B E T A T E S T
R       R     N             O               E     I
S     G L I T C H     S C R O L L     V I R U S
O     I     B     T           L     O               P
R   F   M A I N F R A M E     O N L I N E
            O           A P P     A
F O R T R A N     L O G I N       I N K J E T
```

92 INITIAL HERE AND HERE

93 OH, GODS

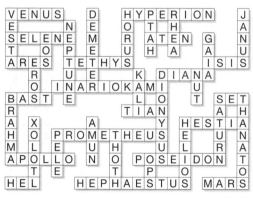

149

94 NAMES FROM FAR, FAR AWAY

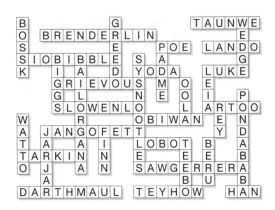

95 JUST MY CUP OF T

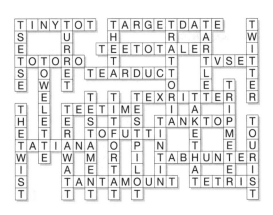

96 GOTTA CATCH 'EM ALL

97 TRIPLE ANAGRAMS

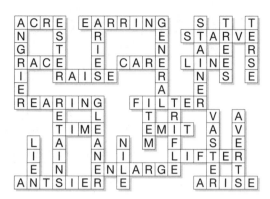

98 NOT ENOUGH VOWELS

99 TOO MANY VOWELS

100 X MARKS THE STOP

101 ALL THE WAY DOWN

102 GETTING EVEN

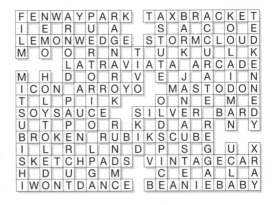

103 THAT'S ODD

```
S E M I S W E E T   S I R L A N C E L O T
P   E   O       W     U E       A   A   O
E A G E R     C L I P B O A R D   J U M B O
A   R   E     O   N   Z   L I     U   P   T
R O Y A L P U R P L E   M A C I N T O S H
A   O     C   E       R       K     I   P
W I N G S   H E A R O U T     V I V A L D I
E       E   P   K       I     A   A     C
S C H E R Z O   S T A N D I N     N O V A K
T   O       T     I   A   D       C   I
W A T E R G A T E   M O L L Y C O D D L E
O   S     U   T   P   L   P   K   U   A   V
R E H A B   O Z O N E H O L E     V O L V O
L   O     L       C   S   O       E   I   K
D O T H E D I S H E S   L O W E R C A S E
```

104 5, 6, 7, 8

```
R O T H K O   F R U I T C U P   S   S
A   I   I     R       E       E L P H A B A
N Y P D B L U E       E       S   Y   L   L
D   J   I     S T A R T R E K   C H I C O
B L A S T     C       H   Y   A   E   E
    R   Z A G A T   S O       I M P R O V
J O S I E     H O N O R       I       E
U       R A F F I   A   G I Z M O       R
I   L         N O K I A       K A F K A
C H A N E L   K   E   N S Y N C   R
E   Z   X   B     K       E   O N E P M
B A Y O U   R A P U N Z E L     R   N   A
A   E   R   A   G         F O U R T E E N
R O Y G B I V   E         I       A   M O
    E   S   O V A L T I N E   S L A Y E R
```

105 AT THE 7-11

```
B O B S B U R G E R S     R I D D L E S
A       E         O   J   O   O       H
T U R N R E D       L   U M A Z U R K A
C       T   I   T R O T S K Y   E   E M
A S P I R I N     R   I   T T W O S T E P
V   I   A   O P O S S U M   H   F   T O
E N Z Y M E S   J   T   A   B U F F A L O
    Z       A   A       R   U       L
P L A T E A U   N   O   R   S P R A Y O N
A   P   A   R   H A R R I E T   I   N I
P R A I R I E   O   G   E   E X T I N C T
A   R   P   G A R L A N D   R   A       P
Y U L E L O G   S   N       S A L I E R I
A   O   U       E   I       I           C
S T R E G I S     C A P T A I N K I R K
```

106 FIVE AND DIME

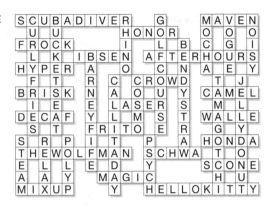

107 10-4, GOOD BUDDY

108 7-10 SPLIT

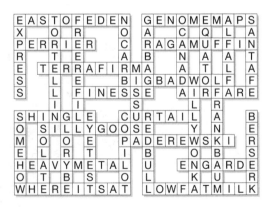

154

109 WORKING 9 TO 5

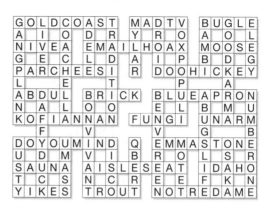

110 GOOD LUCK AND BAD LUCK

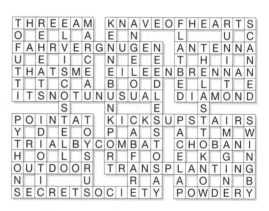

111 2 BY 4

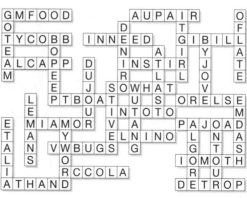

112 SIX-PACK

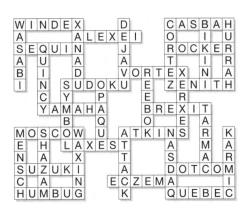

113 THE MAGNIFICENT SEVEN

114 CRAZY EIGHTS

115 CRAZIER EIGHTS

```
S U D D E N L Y         U N G A I N L Y
H   E       A     P       E   L       I
A   A       Z     O T T E R P O P     P
M E L B L A N C   W       O   H       G
E   M       R   O N E N I G H T       L
F U E L C E L L   R       O I L B A R O N
U   I       T   D I S B A N D S   E   S
L I N D Y H O P   A   P   A M E T H Y S T
  P       M   S L O W L E A K   N   O   E
K R A K A T O A       R   O U T O F G A S
  O       S   L Y R I C I S T   I   I   T
  M       U   E       T   B I T B Y B I T
  I       M R M I Y A G I     L   E   U
  S       A   I       F       E   A   B
K E E P C O O L         P E D I G R E E
```

116 THE WHOLE NINE YARDS

```
A S K A R O U N D       V O I C E M A I L
N       I       E       O       N
G I F T O F G A B       T O W E L E T T E
K       G       I   J     A       H
O       R       T R A Y T A B L E   E
R       A       C   M     U       L
W   P E N N Y L A N E   F E N C E D O F F
A   I   D   O   R   S   I   G   Q   O   A
T A X R E F U N D   B U B B A G U M P   C
  I       G       O   O     I       C   E
  E   C R O M A G N O N     P       M   V
  C       G       D   A     M       N   A
L O U D S H I R T       C L O S E C A L L
  T       R             C       N       U
  A S T R O L A B E     I D O N T C A R E
```

117 PERFECT 10

```
J                       P U F F P I E C E S
R A R I N G T O G O     R         O
R       O               M A I D M A R I A N
T O F U H O T D O G     O   G     N
O       S         R O O K I E Y E A R
L   W   E   L   A   D   D   E   E   V
K O A L A B E A R S   I N A B S E N T I A
I   T   U   U   S     N   I   I   U   N
E E C U M M I N G S   D U R A N D U R A N
N   H   P   D   K     I   E   D   N   A
  W E B S U R F I N G     E         W
  O       O   R   O Z Z I E S M I T H
W O R K P E R M I T       D         I
  D           A   U N I C Y C L I S T
J A S M I N E T E A               E
```

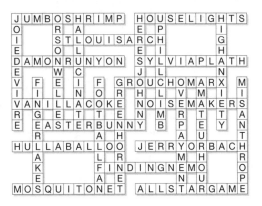

ABOUT THE AUTHOR

FRANCIS HEANEY's puzzles have appeared in *The New York Times*, *The Wall Street Journal*, *Games*, *Wired*, *The Onion*, *Fast Company*, and other publications. He also constructs regularly for the American Values Club Crossword (avxwords.com), and was named Constructor of the Year in 2013 and 2017 in the yearly Orca awards presented by the crossword review blog Diary of a Crossword Fiend.

He is also the author of a whole bunch of puzzle books, including *Mini Acrostics*, *Drunk Crosswords* (with Brendan Emmett Quigley), *Brain Games for Word Nerds*, *Sudoku in Space*, *Sit & Solve Picture Word Search Puzzles*, *Word Search Sudoku* (with Frank Longo), and *Boss Lady Word Search Puzzles*. You might enjoy digging up his collection of anagram-based literary parodies, *Holy Tango of Literature*, out of print but still funny, and readable online if you follow the links at www.francisheaney.com. He often has opinions about puzzles on Twitter (@fheaney).